SCOTLAND LAUGHING

"The sudden intrusion of the droll . . ."

"We'll hiv tae make it a three-ba', Wullie's fit
slipped . . ."

SCOTLAND
LAUGHING

The Humour of the Scot

by

W. B. BURNETT

Illustrations by

GRAHAM

THE ALBYN PRESS

EDINBURGH & LONDON

FIRST PUBLISHED 1955

SECOND EDITION 1956

THIRD EDITION 1958

FOURTH EDITION 1960

FIFTH EDITION 1964

SIXTH EDITION 1969

SEVENTH EDITION 1973

EIGHTH EDITION 1974

THE ALBYN PRESS
3 ABBEYMOUNT
EDINBURGH 8
AND
90 THE BROADWAY
LONDON SW19

Printed in Scotland by
LINDSAY & CO LTD
EDINBURGH

CONTENTS

FOREWORD

IT is surely unnecessary to allude in more than a passing sentence to Sydney Smith's infamous charge that the Scot has no sense of humour—that "it requires a surgical operation to get a joke well into a Scotch understanding." It has already been aptly enough said that we need not be disturbed at this time of day by the report of a Minor Canon.

On the other hand, I feel there will be many ready to agree that it is now more than time that the more familiar specimens of our National Humour were supplemented and presented in a new way, if only to show our increasing numbers of visitors what kind of folk we are. For nothing will give a readier clue to our make-up than samples of what we regard as worth a laugh.

FOREWORD TO LATER EDITIONS

It had been my intention, as later editions went to press, to replace a considerable number of examples in the original selection by others which seemed to me to be stronger in point and character. So many of the specimens which had been noted for exclusion have, however, been quoted with approval by friendly reviewers and others, that I have taken a second thought about many of the proposed changes and my revision has been on a much more limited scale than originally intended.

W. B. B.

1. NATIONAL CHARACTERISTICS

Stands Scotland where it did?

THERE are still some pessimists among us who will insist that in the fast moving world of to-day all things are becoming unified, and that all races are becoming standardised into a kind of grey uniformity. They will tell you that even if there did exist in an earlier day certain qualities and attributes which were accepted as typically Scottish, they have long been covered by the evolutionary tide. We are asked to accept the hard fact that all traces of these traditional and distinctive marks of the Scot have now been lost and forgotten, and that nothing can wile them back. It is an old story.

More than a century ago, Sir Walter Scott was lamenting that the peculiar features of Scottish manners and customs were daily melting and dissolving into those of her sister and ally. Some fifty years later, Dean Ramsay was just as concerned about the changes taking place in his own lifetime. Scotland, he declared, was losing much of the pungent wit and dry humour of sayings in her native dialect. Only the slighter shades of national characteristics remained, and Scottish life was becoming every year less and less distinguished from the rest of the world. What else could be expected if, as Sydney Smith put it, " the Scotsman could eat his porridge in the morning and scratch himself in Piccadilly ere set of sun."

If, reflecting upon the effects of " enlarged intercourse with England and the world " our grandfathers could feel so disturbed, I wonder what they would have to say to-day if they could return to find themselves confronted with the internal combustion engine, the popular press, the unending voice of radio, television and the rest. Imagine their alarm if they could have foreseen that in Perth or Peebles the native would read, hear, and see what was being read and heard and seen in Paris or Pittsburg ; if they had thought it credible that twice a week the morning train would bring California or the African Desert to the village in a tin box ; and that the 'bus to the town would pass the road-end at five past the hour.

Well, it's gude to dread the warst, as the old saying goes, for the best will be the welcomer. Fears are often liars. Nobody will deny that in the process of world shrinkage there have been changes in the domestic and social life of Scotland as elsewhere. But the physical conditions of the country and her unique history of unremitting struggle have, for weal or woe, left their settled marks. Speaking of the gulf separating the Scots and the English, Stevenson saw clearly enough the profound differences in their thoughts and ways. "Not Unions," he declared, "nor mutual dangers, nor steamers, nor railways, nor all the King's horses and all the King's men, seem able to obliterate the broad distinction."

Nature has been a stern foster-mother; every other brae has had its gory bicker. If the schooling has been harsh the gain has been great. But adversity has had its compensations, and it is inevitable that there should remain enduring lines on the spirit of the succeeding race. The specimens of national humour in the following pages ought to be answer enough to those who persist in saying that these accepted influences mean nothing at all in modern Scotland, and should serve also as a reminder to the general reader that in his solid traditional qualities and characteristics the true Scot stands just about where he did. For it can still be said of him, as it was of the young Durward, that he has "plenty of blood, plenty of pride and" (alas) "a right good scarcity of ducats."

2. THE INDEPENDENT SCOT

A race unconquered, by her clime made bold.—Waller.

THE Scot has never been very supple at the knee, and it has always been one of his striking characteristics to regard independence as the first of earthly blessings. His love of liberty has never been subdued. The past has taught him to stand firmly on his own legs and to look the world steadily in the eye. He has " a guid conceit of himsel' " and is quick to resent rebuke or even the mildest criticism.

Let him see, as in the following examples, that he is being unjustly censured or mildly patronised, let him see his own blood, and he is not slow in showing himself as a man with any amount of smeddum, ready always to give answer to any and every man. As Stevenson has it, " he who goes fishing among the Scots with condescension for a bait, will have an empty creel by evening."

The old shepherd was being reproached by the minister about his absence from his usual place in the Kirk.

" I was at Mr Doig's Kirk " was the defence. But the minister was not to be easily placated.

" Well," the minister went on, " I don't care much for this running away to strange kirks—even to hear Mr Doig. How would you like to see *your* sheep straying into strange pastures ? "

" Dod, Sir," came the caustic reply, " I wouldna gie a docken if it was better gress."

Old Mrs MacIntyre had at last consulted the Doctor about " trouble with her stomach." After a careful examination the Doctor assured her that there was nothing to worry about.

" It's just wind, Mrs MacIntyre," said the doctor, " just wind."

But Mrs MacIntyre was not to be snubbed in this way—even by her doctor. She had views of her own.

" Jist wind," she replied, " Jist wind ? De ye no ken it was wind that blew doon the Tay Brig ! "

9

The new minister was also a farmer in a small way and was earning a reputation in the parish for his excessive economies. On his rounds one day he saw Weelum, his ploughman, sitting on the plough handle while the horses took a short rest. Reflecting that time was money, he thought the occasion gave him a long desired opportunity for remonstrance.

" Now Weelum," he said firmly, " would it not be a good plan to have a pair of shears handy to give the hedge a bit clip when the horses are resting ? "

" And dae ye no think Sir," replied Weelum, looking the minister in the eye, " it would be a good plan if ye took a basin o' tatties into the pulpit and gied them a bit peel when the choir was at the Anthem ? "

A young servant lassie was being considered for a situation at the farm when she was brusquely informed by the farmer that she would need to produce a reference from her previous employer. Some time later the farmer saw her again and asked her if she now had her " character."

" Ay," she replied, " —but I've gotten yours as weel—and I'm no' comin'."

A well-known Highland Regiment had acquired a widespread and well-merited reputation during the War for exemplary conduct both in and out of action. Among their almost legendary virtues was included the regularity of their letters home, a subject on which they were unmercifully chaffed by the other troops in the locality.

One night as the Scots were coming out of the line they were met by a London regiment and the usual exchanges began.

" I hope you have written your old ' mither ' tonight Jock " shouted one of the Sassenachs, to the accompaniment of loud guffaws from his fellows.

" Ay, ay," returned Jock quietly, " But dae ye never write yersel' ? "

" Sure, Jock, sure," replied the cockneys, " three times a day after meals."

" Aweel," returned Jock with a glint in his eye, " the next time you write, mind and tell her you've seen the sodgers ! "

" He has a guid conceit o' himsel' . . ."

" . . . and now tae conclude, a few simple verses o' ma ain . . ."

As a "man o' independent mind" he is always ready to stand up for his own opinions and is not easily shaken by the pronouncements of the reputed authorities. He is no believer in second-hand judgments, but is determined to do his own thinking and to arrive at his own conclusions.

Sandy was an old weaver with a reputation in the village as a student of theology. In the course of one heated discussion, St. Paul was quoted against him to refute his argument. But the old man was not to be shaken.

"Weel, weel," he replied doggedly. "It's true enough he did say that. But, ye see, that's jist where me and Paul differs!"

Even in his prayers there was an intimidating note. "Lord give us grace," the prayer would go, "For if Thou give us not grace, we shall not give Thee glory—and who will win by that, Lord?" No-one could imagine any but a Scot venturing to say in a prayer "We thank Thee Lord for all Thy Mercies—such as they are!" And only a Scots youth would admit being a member of a Debating Society just to be able to "contradict a wee." And was it not a Scot who suggested that the "NOT" in the Commandments might, after all, be a printer's error?

It is not difficult to see that in this imperfect workaday world a sturdy spirit of independence can only too readily develop into a kind of unbending and cross-grained obstinacy. That uncomfortable but distinctively Scots word "Thrawn" has not been prominent in the language without reason. Listen to him again:—

Old Jimmie had been a dour customer during the greater part of his life. He was the first to find fault with everything. Nothing ever pleased him.

In due course he died and found himself in Heaven. He was joined later by an old crony from his own town.

"Weel, Jimmie," said the newcomer, "there'll no be much to complain aboot here!"

"What!" returned Jimmie like a shot, pointing to the crown on his head, "D'ye ca' that a richt fit?"

The village joiner was nearing his end. The family were all in attendance, and it seemed clear to all that the old man was finally breathing his last. Controlling her emotion, his wife ventured to mention the question of funeral arrangements to her eldest son.

"We'll better jist get Lachie Morrison for everything. Your father and him werena sae very freen'ly but . . ."

She was interrupted by a voice from the bed. Raising himself on his elbow, stubborn to the last, he managed to say,

"Git that craitur Morrison to make the coffin if ye like. But if ye dae, *I'll* no pit a fit in't."

This can perhaps be capped by a similar story coming from Loch Tayside. The old man was dying and the relatives were again discussing the funeral arrangements when suddenly an emphatic voice was heard from the bed.

"I tell ye, I will *not* be buried in that auld shroud in the Kist! Either a new shroud frae Killin or *I'll no dee at a'*!"

A glance at the records suggests that in some parts of the country a feud was indeed a feud. There is, for instance, the well worn case of the old shepherd on his deathbed being implored by his Minister to seek reconciliation with his life-long enemy, and to agree that there should be a meeting between the two warriors before the end.

At last the meeting was arranged at the bedside. Hand-shakes were exchanged, peace was restored, and the Minister beamed approval. The visitors were quietly tiptoeing out of the room when they were stopped by a quavering voice from the bed,

"Noo mind, Donald! If I dinna dee efter a', it's jist tae be atween you an' me as it was afore!"

So strong and so persistent has been this independent note in the character, that there are many ready to say that it has been indulged to excess and that the fervid Scot is far too insistent in his reminders that "Must" was buried at Bannock-burn. They complain that in asserting his freedom he is much too aggressive. A man can be a man for a' that and use elbows just a little less.

Can we wholly dismiss a charge of this kind as a weak invention of the enemy? Or are we bound to admit that there has always been some ground for the reproach? Well, we can't reform our forefathers; and if a partial admission must be made, it is surely not surprising that after centuries of the woes and pains of oppression and lawlessness, something flinty should make its appearance in the national temper. You cannot blame the cobbler if his thumbs are black.

There is probably some foundation for this view that, on occasion, he can be unduly angular, as we recall instances like the following :—

On one of the old Clyde steamers, the man at the wheel was being pestered by the stupid questions of a pompous lady tourist. He answered all her questions briefly but patiently for a long time, indicating quite clearly by the curtness of his manner that she was seriously hindering him in his responsible work.

The passenger refused, however, to desist and haughtily continued with her cross-examination until, losing his temper, the sailor turned on her and—in language coloured by the warmth of his feelings—told her exactly where she (and all her kindred) could go.

In great indignation she immediately reported the matter to the Captain, who did all he could to conciliate her, promising that he would see that his subordinate offered her an ample apology for his conduct and the violence of his language.

Somewhat mollified, the tourist thereupon retired to the Saloon and proceeded with some agitation to recount her experience to her fellow passengers. Just as she was finishing the narrative, a burly figure in dripping oilskins appeared at the Saloon door and called over to his former tormentor to make the *amende honorable*.

" Are you the leddy I tell't t' gang tae blazes ? "

The lady nodded, and awaited the promised apology.

" Weel," continued the sailor, " the Captain says ye needna bother ! "

The gossips in the village had it that Geordie Fleming's daughter had become engaged to a certain young man in the same parish. They also passed on the news to all it might concern that Geordie did not approve of his daughter's choice.

In due course the news of Geordie's opposition reached the ears of the young man's mother. She would have no nonsense from Geordie Fleming, and challenged him when next she met him, returning from the Bowling Green with some of his cronies.

In a towering rage she demanded to know whether he had ever said that her son was not good enough for his daughter.

" I said nae such thing, wummin ! " said Geordie quietly, " A' I said was that he was a hawk oot o' a bad nest ! "

Take also, as another choice example of the thrawn Scot, the case of the young student at a famous University.

The class was a large one and the incident occurred at the end of a long and difficult day. The lecture had taken its normal course, but in his final summary the Professor found it necessary to refer to the translation of a passage read by a comparatively new student and to mention the errors that had occurred.

The student was undeterred by this unexpected criticism and stubbornly defended his own rendering. The Professor, with what patience he could muster, informed him again that his translation had been quite wrong. Still unrepentant, the student continued to insist that *he* was right.

At this point, the Professor lost his patience entirely, and told the interrupter sharply that his conduct could not be tolerated.

" This is most irregular," he said finally. " You will sit down and stop this arguing immediately ! "

" Stop it yersel'," came the aggrieved reply. " Wha started it ? "

Nor is it to be expected that he has much patience with any kind of affectation. It follows that when occasion demands there is always a certain pungency in his speech.

A story in this connection is told of an eminent professor who had been endeavouring for some months to arrange for the visit of one of his colleagues to dinner until his patience was about exhausted. Finally a definite date was arranged but the gentleman informed him that he would come " if he was spared."

" Weel, weel," was the rejoinder, " if ye're deid we'll no' expect ye ! "

After maintaining for so long a time this spirit of self-reliance and independence, the Scot now finds himself typifying the rugged stubborn individualist. He does not, as Stevenson puts it, humbly say Amen to everything the world may tell him. He cannot be relied upon meekly to do or say the conventional or obvious as in an example of this kind.

Andra, an old St. Andrews cabbie, had a weekly order to take a rather voluble lady of uncertain age to one or other of her afternoon Bridge engagements, the arrangement being that the cab waited for the return journey.

One hot summer day, Andra was kept waiting rather longer than usual and was quietly dozing in his dicky seat when he was hailed by one of his cronies.

" Losh, Andra," he shouted, " are ye aye waitin' here yet ? "

" Ay," Andra called back, " I've been standin' at this door for twa hoors waitin' for the bletherin' auld besom."

As luck would have it, the windows of the house were wide open and Andra's remarks were clearly heard by his " fare " inside. In great indignation she at last entered the cab and informed Andra that she would report his conduct to his employer that very day.

In due course the employer heard her story at great length and with a wealth of detail from her flowing tongue.

At length he interrupted the complainer to remark : " Ay, Ay ! And ye tell me he called you a bletherin' auld besom ? "

" Yes," was the reply, " these were his very words."

" Weel, weel," replied the employer, " I'll speak to Andra aboot this. It's nane o' his business *what* ye are ! "

3. THE UNDEMONSTRATIVE SCOT

Fond are our hearts
Although we do not bare them.
             Neil Munro—*The Exiles.*

IF, said R. L. S., a man is lucky enough to be born a Scot, he must pay for the privilege like any other advantage. He must be ready to contend with a variety of charges not the least being that he is unemotional, stolid, and cold.

As the saying goes, wherever there's reek there's heat. Like Dominie Sampson he may perhaps have too much of the " admirable virtue of taciturnity." It may be an over-statement to talk of dourness ; but there is no denying that one conspicuous Scottish characteristic is a deep-rooted distrust of anything savouring of effusiveness or " gush." Like the auld wife's parrot " he doesna' speak muckle but is a deevil to think."

Whether or not the bareness and repressive rigour of his religious upbringing have taught the Scot to be on his guard at the first signs of emotion, the fact remains that he is profoundly uncomfortable at any outward show of affection. " Love ye ? " they will ask in Thrums, " Wheest ! What kin' o' word's that to mak use o'—and folk a' weel enough ? "

We find a typical example of this stiff reserve in the familiar story of the happily married couple on the occasion of their silver wedding. John certainly remembered that this special event called for special measures and he had brought home an attractive piece of jewellery for his wife as a memento.

He fumbled about with it in his pocket for some time, but at last laid it on the table and pushed it in an offhand way towards his wife. Opening the box, his wife expressed her delight at the gift and, her eyes filling with tears, exclaimed :

" O John, it's real bonny. And does this mean that you love me just as much as ever ? "

John looked a trifle watery in the eye too, but could only allow himself as reply " Ay ! seemin'ly."

This recalls the story of the Scots wife who had been visiting her husband in the Infirmary. She was so relieved at the prospect of his recovery that she was moved to say to him as she was preparing to leave,

" Would you like me to kiss ye before I go dearie ? "

" Wud ye daur ! " at once came the horrified reply.

Even if, in an unguarded moment, he should forget to conceal his true feelings, he loses no time in resuming his guard.

Old John had been confined to bed for many weary weeks. One fine spring morning his pretty auburn-haired nurse arrived with his morning tea. As she pulled up the blind, the sunshine lit up her hair and she was indeed " a sicht for sair een."

" Eh nurse," John was moved to say, " but you're lookin' real bonny this morning—unless it's me no seein' richt ! "

Let the alien detractor have his smile. But he makes a sad mistake if, judging by externals, he concludes that the Scot has no heart because he does not wear one on his sleeve. For, as Chesterton has noticed, the truth is that the Scot is a secret sentimentalist—but he has difficulty in keeping the secret. Behind the mask of indifference and the hard surface of his reserve he is fighting grimly to conceal his true feelings, even at the very end of things.

An old worthy was on his death bed and his wife was reminding him that for fifty years he had brought her a cup of tea in the morning.

" What will I dae," she asked, " when you're no' here to bring it up to me ? "

" Och," came the staid reply, " ye can get a wee gas ring ! "

In this connection Sir Harry Lauder used to tell the story of the Deeside wife who had listened for a whole evening to his jokes and patter without a hint of a smile. The next day, however, she confided to a friend " He's a great comic. It was a' I could dae to keep frae laughin'."

The reticence and caution of years now find him with the capacity to maintain control over his emotions. Experience has now left him with a kind of sober and composed commonsense and he goes about the world with a merited reputation for imperturbability. He is not easily upset or excited. In a word he can keep " a calm sough " as in a case of this kind :

THE UNDEMONSTRATIVE SCOT

" He has a merited reputation for imperturbability . . ."

The train was on the point of moving out of the Waverley Station in Edinburgh, when a Fife miner entered the compartment until then occupied by a lady passenger.

She had her cosmetics all carefully arranged on the opposite seat and intended to improve the shining hour by undertaking some personal decoration. She made it quite clear to the intruder that she was extremely annoyed at his unexpected appearance and at last exclaimed :

" Do you know, my man, I am just recovering from a very severe attack of scarlet fever, and it will be very dangerous for you to travel in this compartment ? "

" Dinna worry aboot me, lassie," replied the Fifer, " I'm cutting my throat in the Haymarket Tunnel."

Choice instances of imperturbality are often provided from the North-West.

One of these concerns the Stornoway fisherman who was working on a Drifter in the Minch, quietly smoking his pipe, when, in a sudden squall, he was thrown overboard. It was only with the greatest difficulty and after a long struggle that he was finally rescued, more dead than alive.

As his drenched body lay on deck, it was noticed that his pipe was still tightly clenched between his teeth. Reviving slightly, he put his hand to his mouth, removed and examined his pipe and calmly announced, without sign of emotion, " It's oot ! "

There is, too, the classic example of Scots composure in the reply of Mrs Baird, on receiving the news that her son— who later became General Sir David Baird—was a prisoner in the hands of Hyder Ali. " Lord help the chiel that's chained tae oor Davie " was her only comment.

It cannot be overlooked that this staid self-possession can on occasion develop into something which can hardly be accounted a merit, as we encounter examples like the following :

Old Andrew had lost his wife and was returning from the funeral with some of his relatives. They were a very sombre company and many were the expressions of sympathy for the old man in his great loss.

"Weel, weel," he sighed as he entered the empty house, "forty-six years is a lang time. She was a guid wife to me. A grand cook and a guid hoosekeeper. Ay, ay, she looked weel efter me."

"But," he turned and added after a pause, "d'ye ken, *I never liked her !*"

We can also recall the familiar—if extreme—example from the old sheep-stealing days.

A Highland sheep-farmer had sent off his son to Falkirk market with a flock ; and as was the not uncommon practice of those days, there were sundry unauthorised additions to the flock in the course of the journey. In the sequel, in this case, the culprit was discovered and duly hanged at Perth for sheep stealing.

The father waited for some weeks for the return of the prodigal before venturing to make any enquiry. Finally he approached one of his neighbours.

"By the bye," he began after a few exchanges about weather and prices, "you were at Falkirk, I wouldn't wonder. Did you see anything of our Donald ? "

"Oh yes, by the bye," replied the other, "I saw him on the gallows at Perth."

"Do you tell me that now," replied the father with no outward sign of emotion, "it would be for sheeps I'se warrant. I always thocht it would be for sheeps."

But, it is also claimed, he is able to keep "an ever tranquil mind " in good as well as evil fortune. There was for instance the Scot in America who received a visit one day from an excited Pressman with the news that he had won first prize in a large Newspaper Competition. The first prize, the agitated visitor informed him, was ten thousand dollars, a new house, a motor car, and a pet dog.

But the winner showed no visible signs of elation, his only rejoinder being, " What breed ? "

The reference made during the War to the young Scots soldier who said nothing to his wife about winning the V.C. because " it wasna his turn to write," recalls the familiar case of Willie McBean, V.C., who showed that Scottish composure as well as Scottish courage mounteth with occasion.

Willie, although he died with the rank of Major-General, joined the old 93rd Highlanders as a private soldier, and while in the ranks was awarded his V.C. at Lucknow for disposing, single-handed, of no fewer than eleven mutineers. At the decoration ceremony, the officiating General, on pinning the Cross on Willie's breast, made the usual speech of congratulation and commended him very highly before the assembled Regiment for what he described as " a good day's work."

But this was hardly good enough for the composed and collected Willie. " Hoots, man," he corrected, " the hale thing didnae tak me twenty meenites."

Even on sporting occasions he will exhibit this ability to remain unruffled and detached when his neighbours are in a state of agitation.

The scene was Hampden Park and the great International between Scotland and England was nearing its close. There was a wildly enthusiastic crowd and excitement was at fever pitch when a penalty was awarded to Scotland.

In the sudden hush before the vital kick was taken, a voice in a broad Buchan accent was heard to exclaim :

" Man, is this no a grand growin' day ! "

Humorous examples of this calm unconcern are also common in the records of exchanges in the courts. The nervous witness is all too often the cause of " laughter in court," but the average Scot is not very easily overawed by the importance of the occasion. This is especially the case where the witness is " in from the country."

Counsel had been cross-examining a shepherd from one of the outlying parishes and had, with malice aforethought, put to him a long and confusing question.

After a prolonged pause, during which counsel's smile broadened, the silence was at last broken. " Would ye mind," asked the shepherd with quiet deliberation, " Would ye mind jist repeatin' that question and splittin' it intae sma' bits ? "

In the lower courts particularly—where some local tie frequently binds judge and judged—many similar humorous exchanges have occurred, underlining this mark of imperturbability.

There was, for instance, the case of the Bailie who was sitting in judgment for the first time and anxious to show that he took his new duties with becoming gravity. When the proceedings commenced it was found that one of the witnesses was inclined to treat the Court with a certain levity.

After some consultation, the Bailie was ultimately advised to warn the offender that he would commit him for contempt of Court if he did not conduct himself in a proper manner.

" The Coort—wha's the Coort," asked the witness.

" *I* am the Court," replied the Bailie with dignity.

" Troth, and ye're naething o' the kind," came the reply, " ye're auld Dod Scott the plumber."

Even when his final hour has come, Scottish composure is not too seriously shaken. Indeed, it is in this extremity that it may be fairly said of him, as Carlyle said of Scott, that he is a " most composed and invincible man."

The old Scottish blacksmith on his deathbed was receiving what he realised was a final visit from his minister. Seeing that the old man was anxious to say something, the visitor asked him to speak freely if anything was troubling him. Eyeing the clerical vest which buttoned at the side, the old smith was anxious to solve at least one mystery before he went.

" Weel, it's jist this, Sir ; I canna for the life o' me see how ye managed to get into that waistcoat."

THE THRIFTY SCOT

"He has never been able to tolerate waste . . ."

4. THE THRIFTY SCOT

A sillerless man gaes fast through the market.
—Scots Proverb.

IT has been said that Poverty is the first fact in the history of Scotland. It follows that the Scot, coming from a long line of forebears blessed with but little material wealth, has never been able to tolerate waste in any form. Show him the majesty of the Pyramids, and he asks " What damned eediot biggit thae things ? " Put him down on the banks of Niagara and his main concern is for the " perfect waste o' water."

In a country in which it has been " ill to gether gear " he has had to make the most of hard circumstances and—if he was to survive—to remember always to ask his purse what he could buy. For many a day he has known too well that for every Five Pound Note there was ever a Ten Pound Road and that only by saving comes having. He never pays cash without reflection. In a word, thrift is in his blood. As the cynic has it " A Mactavish is never lavish."

Thus, over the years, prudence and thrift have come to be regarded as peculiarly Scottish characteristics. It was, however, from this somewhat sombre background that there emerged within comparatively recent years the grotesque myth, now almost a world myth, of Scottish Meanness. To an Englishman, it is said, money is round that it may roll. To a Scot, it is flat, that it may lie still. With just the necessary grain of truth to give colour to the caricature, it has for a time been the fashion to portray the Scot as a niggardly, grudging tightfist, a " grippy man wi' sillar "—a man who will only cast his bread upon the waters if the tide is coming in.

At this time of day nothing much need be said about this libel beyond reminding the stage Scotsman that he has most of the answering to do. The earlier versions of the sour legend had no doubt the appeal of novelty and may even yet provoke a wintry smile—the banging o' saxpences (on wine and cigars), the moths in purses, the sillar in ma ither pocket, and the rest of them. But, by the most crude and obvious effort over the years, Scots " Comics " have toiled and sweated to expand and elaborate the grisly theme to almost revolting limits.

There are, of course, fashions in Humour as in other things ; and fortunately fashions of any kind have no very deep roots. But having seen the present vogue degenerating, as 'Stephen Leacock has put it, into " mere brutality," a change is surely overdue.

The Aberdonian himself, while superficially keeping up the legend, is beginning to show some signs of impatience, and his rejoinders can be pungent enough when occasion demands.

The scene was the lounge of an Aberdeen hotel, and a party of English commercial travellers were airing their views about the meanness of the Scot. At last, with the intention of giving colour to his opinions, the leader of the group approached an Aberdonian at the adjoining table with the question :—

" Can you tell me the difference between an Aberdonian and a cocoanut ? "

With a hint of steel in his eye, the Aberdonian quietly shook his head.

" Well," said the Englishman, " You can get a drink out of a cocoanut."

All round guffaws followed.

" No bad, man, no bad," replied the Scot, nettled, but still smiling. " And could *you* dae wi' a drink noo ? "

Thinking he had goaded the Scot into unwonted generosity, the Englishman at once replied.

" Yes, thanks, I do need a drink."

" Weel," was the crisp reply, " Awa' and buy a cocoanut ! "

Listen to the Scot declaring that somebody is " No worth a damn—unless you're sweirin' onywey," and you are getting a hint of what is meant by the economical Scot. The alien observer, however, has not yet begun to see that if the Scot is as careful with his money as with his words it is only that he may have it ready for the " glorious privilege " of being materially independent of others and of using it at what he considers the proper time, and for something *he* considers worth while. He knows all too well that money is hard to come by, and does not, with Johnson, call a tree generous that sheds its fruit at every breeze. He has learned that if he puts nothing in his purse he can take nothing out.

Let these examples speak. They could only originate in a land where prudence and thrift are marked features of the national character.

The famous Scottish singer, David Kennedy, has recalled the day his worthy father gave him three bawbees to spend at the village fair.

"You are at liberty to spend it a', David," his father assured him, "but the less you spend the more I will think o' ye!"

During the heavy and terrible Clydeside Blitz, poor old Mrs Blair was sitting alone in her kitchen when suddenly the house crashed about her ears. Several hours elapsed before the rescue squad found her lying covered by the debris and more dead than alive.

When at last she was dragged from the ruins, she was asked if she had any spirits in the house.

"There's whisky," she managed to gasp, "it's—it's in the press!"

Miraculously, the bottle was finally discovered in what remained of the kitchen press.

"It's a mercy we found this, Mrs Blair," said the returning Warden. "Now here you are! Ye can dae wi' it!"

Mrs Blair looked at the bottle but turned away her head.

"Na, Na!" she whispered at last, "that's for an emergency!"

John, who was getting on in years had unexpectedly been appointed bellman in the Parish Kirk much to the surprise and delighted satisfaction of his wife. She made no secret of her pleasure and lost no time in advising all and sundry of the good news.

"Have ye heard o' the grand job ma man has jist gotten," she asked her neighbours.

"No," replied one, "what is it?"

"The ringin' o' the Kirk bell," replied the proud wife.

"And whatna wage comes wi' that?" came the vital question.

"Oh, he's weel paid," said Mrs John, "he gets £5 a year and *a free grave*!"

Andrew was a great hand at odd jobs about the house. One day he found it necessary to call at the home of his friend and neighbour on a small matter of business. His knock was answered by his friend's wife.

" Is Wullie, in ? " asked the visitor.

" Ay he's in," was the reply.

" Weel, can I see him," continued the caller.

" No ye canna see him," returned the wife.

" But I want to see him on a bit o' business," persisted Andrew.

" Weel, ye canna see him.   He's deid ! " came the announcement from the door.

" Was it sudden ? " asked Andrew.

" Ay very sudden," he was informed.

" Weel," continued Andrew, " did he say onything aboot a pot o' green pent before he slippit awa' ? "

Even in moments of emotional excitement he can be sufficiently guarded and careful to avoid what he regards as foolish extravagance.

There is on record the case of the town neer-do-weel who publicly announced his conversion during a local religious revival.   Among his many known weaknesses swearing and tobacco-chewing were prominent ; and when the time came for him to give his personal testimony, he proudly avowed that he had not used *one* swear word for a whole week.   As if that were not merit enough, he also announced that he would stop chewing tobacco—" as soon as the wee bit o' black twist in his pocket was finished."

If the reader believes that in these and similar suggestions of rigid thrift and frugality he finds all the justification necessary for the legend of meanness, it can only be said that he knows but little of Scotland's story.   But a few familiar illustrations in lighter vein ought to show that if the Scot is proverbially poor and proud no one, as Hazlitt has said, need after all be sorry for him.   If he cannot always remedy his poverty, when he sets about it he has an eye for a bargain and can at least see that he gets value for money.

The scene is a tramway stop in the famous Union Street, and Mrs Gordon, firmly holding her grandchild by the hand, is in conversation with the conductor.

" Hoo much is't to Mannofield ? " she asked.

" Tuppence to Mannofield," she was informed.

" An hoo much for him ? " she asked again, with a nod towards the child.

" O, it's nothing for the likes o' him," explained the conductor.

" Aweel, in that case," came the reply, " jist pit the laddie off at Mannofield. I'm walkin'! "

We are, of course, still in Aberdeen. It was a cold January night and a weary Willie had been tramping the streets all day but had not been able to obtain the wherewithal for his night's lodging.

At last, in desperation, he climbed to the top flat of a tenement, knocked at the door, and asked the guid wife if she could spare 2d. for a bed.

" Weel," she replied after considering the situation for a moment, " bring it up and we'll see what it's like ! "

The meeting of commercial travellers had been organised to inaugurate a league for the abolition of tipping. Andrew was there but was showing no great enthusiasm for the project. At length the Chairman addressed him personally.

" Surely, Mr MacIntyre, you are going to join us ? After all, the subscription is only one shilling a year ! "

" A shilling a year ? " returned the wide-awake Andrew. " At that rate, I micht as weel keep on tipping ! "

The scene again is not a hundred miles from Union Street, and Andrew is taking leave of his brother bound for the south.

" Now, Andra," said the traveller from the carriage window, " if anything should happen to Grannie when I'm away, you should, I think, send me a wire." There was a pause before he added " And dinna forget that you get twelve words for sixpence."

All the last minute instructions were duly observed and in due course Andra's message arrived :—

" MACKAY "—OTEL, LONDON. GRANNIE PASSED AWAY TODAY. ABERDEEN 2, DUNDEE 1. ANDREW."

The Practical Scot

"A severely practical man."

5. THE PRACTICAL SCOT

But facts are chiels that winna ding—Burns.

IT has been said that there are as many sides to the Scottish character as there are checks in a plaid. History, climate, and physical features have combined to produce the proverbially undemonstrative and thrifty Scot with his strongly developed sense of independence. But there are other equally prominent features in his make-up; and all the reliable estimates of the character of the Scot portray him also as a severely practical man, competent and hard-headed.

In moving about his world, he is concerned primarily with the practical use of things. When the Fifer was shown St. Paul's for the first time his only comment was, " Man, it would haud a terrible lot o' hay." And when the Forfar Bailie was asked to express an opinion about the Pyramids his summing up was simply, " Losh! Whatna rowth o' mason work and nae rent comin' in."

There is a pungency and penetration in much of his humour, confirming that first and last he is a realist, with a homely grip on fact.

" Me an elder ? " asked the old farmer. " Me an elder ? Hoo could a' be an elder an' sell a horse ? "

This severely practical aspect of the character comes out in instances like these :

" And how is your new Minister getting on ? " the villager was asked.

" O fine, I think," was the reply, " but he's hardly settled doon yet."

" But they tell me he is one o' the kind that disna believe in Hell."

" Aweel," came the grim rejoinder, " He'll no be here long afore he changes his mind."

" We'll no' pray for rain the day, brethren," announces the pulpit realist, " the glass is ower high ! "—a remark which later evokes from one of his congregation the blunt matter-of-fact comment : " Ay ! Catch him praying for rain for my neeps and his hay no' in yet."

A young servant lassie had been sent from the farm-house to draw water from the nearby burn, but returned, drenched to the skin, after an unusually long absence. Her anxious mistress immediately asked her where she had been and what had kept her.

" What keepit me did ye' say ! " replied the lassie. " 'Deed, I'm lucky to be here at a'. The burn was in spate, I missed ma fit and in I fell, pitcher and a' ; and if it hadna' been for Providence *and another wuman*, I'd hae been drooned ! "

The day of the funeral had come and gone and the old widow was receiving a visit of condolence from some of her friends in the village who were reminding her that brief life was here our portion.

" It's jist the wey o' the world, Mrs McKay," said one of them putting in her word of comfort. " Here today and gone tomorrow ! "

" Ay ! " was the matter-of-fact reply, " jist like a bloomin' circus ! "

Andra had been busy for a long time in clearing some very rough ground as an extension to his garden.

After months of toil he was at last seeing some of the fruits of his labours and, with pardonable pride, was admiring the display of blooms and vegetables when the Minister approached with a smile of approval.

" Well Andra," he began, " I must say that you and the Creator between you have done a grand job on this ground."

But Andra was not too pleased about the division of credit.

" Maybe so," he replied, " maybe so—but you should have seen it when the Creator had it a' tae Himsel'."

An old Border woman, worn out after a lifetime of over-work, had taken to her bed at last. The Minister was making what he regarded as a death-bed visit. He was, of course, familiar with her life-story of unremitting toil and was endeavouring to comfort her by the assurance that she would soon be enjoying the rest she had so richly earned.

But, after her life's experience in a hard School, she could not easily believe that there could ever be such a thing as rest for *her*.

"Weel, Minister," came the severely practical reply, "I doot if I dee the nicht, the Resurrection will be the morn's mornin'!"

It was pay night. And the two cronies, Rob and Andra, had had a drop too much to drink. What had started as a friendly argument had ended in blows. Rob had been taken home for urgent repairs, but Andra had followed him " to come oot-side and fecht it oot."

While Rob's wounds were given some attention by his wife, Andra continued to shout his loud invitations to " come oot and no' be a coo'ard." At last Mrs Rob could stand it no longer. " Awa' oot and feenish him," she encouraged—but with characteristic forethought she added, " but be sure ye dinna break the floor-pot at the front door."

As in the case of other national characteristics, this strictly matter-of-fact outlook begins to show itself at an early age.

The Bible lesson had been about the story of Joseph and Mary.

The teacher had given the children a graphic account of the hardships of the father and mother and how, to crown all, they could find no room in the Inn and had in the end been forced to take refuge in a manger. The sad story had made a deep impression on at least one member of the class and he thought hard about it all the following week.

At the commencement of the next Scripture lesson he raised his hand.

" Well, Andrew," asked the teacher, " what is it now?"

" Please, miss," enquired the sympathetic Andrew, " is there ony word o' yon folk that were lookin' for a hoose?"

It could have been the same severely practical young realist who, on being asked what he thought life would be like in a land flowing with milk and honey, promptly replied " awfu' sticky!"

There is another familiar case of the young Scot who shewed his true Scottishness at a very early age.

On his journey to school it was seldom he met anyone. One day, however, he did see a lone figure approaching, and later discovered he had met the Parish Minister. The Minister stopped and greeted the boy, making the usual enquiries about his progress at school. As he was about to move on, the Minister put his final question.

" And now, my little man " he asked kindly, " and what might your name be? "

" Surely, Sir " replied the matter of fact young Scot, " surely ye havenae forgotten me already? Man, ye baptized me! "

The class at school were being taught the parables and, as a novelty, were allowed to act them in a series of short sketches. When the minister paid one of his periodical visits he asked Wattie—who happened to be in the front row—which of the parables he liked the best.

" The prodigal son," was the prompt reply.

" Well," said the minister, " in that case we'll just have that one acted to-day."

" No, sir," continued Wattie firmly, " we canna dae it the day."

" And why not, my boy? " enquired the visitor.

" Weel," answered Wattie with a glance at the vacant seat beside him, usually occupied by the fatted calf, " ye see, sir, the coo's at the clinic! "

Wee Andrew was brought up on a farm, but the day at last came for his first attendance at school.

As the day wore on, he missed the usual activities of the farm. At last, he stretched his arms, yawned and rose from his seat in the class.

" What's wrong, Andrew? " asked the teacher, " are you wearying? "

" No," replied the practical Andrew, " but I'll need to be getting awa' hame for I've some threshing to dae."

One day, at a later stage of his young career, he was making very poor progress with his rice pudding, and his mother was doing all she could to encourage him to empty his plate.

As a final inducement, she reminded him that, in China, there were millions and millions of children who would be thankful for even a small plate of rice.

But the matter-of-fact Andrew was not yet convinced.

" Weel," he challenged, " name one o' them! "

It seems certain that the young Watties and Andrews and their kind will one day justify Carlyle's description of the Scot as a most shrewd, observing and quietly discerning man. With his orderly and logical cast of mind, he probes doggedly for reasons and the practical justification for things. He must know all the whys and wherefores. The superficial answer is not enough. He is relentless and persistent in his pursuits of the facts.

During the stay of a travelling mission in a small town in the North East, one of the preachers stopped a native in the street and asked him why he did not patronise the meetings.

"Weel, man," came the reply, "there's ae thing I'd like tae ken first and it's this—where dae ye come frae ? "

"Oh," replied the preacher, "I come from the Lord."

"Aye, aye, jist that—but wha sent ye ? " the native went on.

"It was the Lord who sent me," was the reply.

But this was not good enough for the matter-of-fact Scot.

"Na, na, man, that's no' what I mean. What I want tae ken is, *wha' peys ye* ? "

We are often reminded that on the outside cover of all copies of the Shorter Catechism it was the practice to print a multiplication table, and that thus the Scot inevitably finds himself belonging not only to a godly but also to a calculating nation. Even the Minister and the Elder, it appears, have some difficulty in escaping the reproach.

One Sabbath morning, at the conclusion of the Service, Minister and Elder met at the Kirk door.

"If this had been Monday, John," began the Minister, "I might have asked ye about the hay prices at the Friday Market."

John was in no way surprised at this method of approach.

"Weel," he replied, "if this hadna' been the Lord's day I would have said it was the same as the week afore."

"Are you telling me that now ? " went on the Minister. "Well, if this had not been the day it is, I would have mentioned to you that I have some to sell."

"Ay, ay," returned John with a far-away look in his eye, "is that so ? Well now, if this had been a Monday as ye say, I would just have said that I would gie you the day's price for a' ye hae."

The subject was abruptly changed—but John's cart was at the Manse door next day.

"Each new impression only deepens the desire of native places . . ."

" Man, it's gran' tae be back in Scotland . . ."

6. THE LOYAL SCOT

O Scotia, my dear, my native soil.—Burns.

OF the varied elements constituting the character of the Scot, it can be claimed with some assurance that loyalty is perhaps the most conspicuous. He is nothing if not patriotic. His proverbial love of country not only binds him more closely to his native town, village or glen, but also expresses itself in extreme loyalty to kith and kin. Scott has left us the authentic picture.

" You do not know the genius of that man's (Rob Roy's) country, Sir," said Rashleigh Osbaldistone. " Ardent patriotism forms as it were the outmost of the concentric bulwarks with which a Scotsman fortifies himself . . . Surmount this mound, you find an inner and still dearer barrier—the love of his province, his village, or most probably, his clan ; storm this second obstacle, you have a third—his attachment to his own family, his father, mother, sons, daughters, uncles, aunts, and cousins to the ninth generation."

It is always with obvious relish that Scott reminds us of this innermost bulwark. " Your Grace kens we Scotch are clannish bodies," said Mrs Glass to the Duke of Argyle. " Bluid's thicker than water," declared the worthy Mr Nicol Jarvie, " and it lies na in kith, kin or ally to see motes in ilk others e'en if other e'en see them no." And Andrew Fairservice felt he could quickly reassure his companions in announcing that his " mither's mither's third cousin was cousin to the Provost of Dumfries, and he winna see a drap o' her bluid wranged."

There are many recorded examples underlining this distinctive Scottish trait. " Efter a'," said the widow on being condoled on the loss of her husband, " Efter a', he wisna a drap's bluid kin to me."

This reply recalls the domestic problem of the Borderer whose sister had been living with his wife and himself for many years. But two women is " one ower mony " in any house and finally the situation could be endured no longer. One of the women must leave. But bluid was bluid and kin was kin— and his wife went.

" What did ye expect ? " he asked with some surprise, " put away my ain sister for a strange wummin ? "

He has always been vitally, some would say clannishly, interested in his ain folk. Dr Johnson himself was one of those who complained of the inveterate disposition of Scotsmen to sustain the honour of their country at whatever cost, and to stand together through fair weather and foul. " A Scotsman must be a sturdy moralist," he declared, " who does not love Scotland better than the truth." And there are times when there does seem to be some ground for the taunt.

Let the London Policeman and others explain.

The motorist in London had overturned a fruit-hawker's barrow, apples were scattered all over the street, and the Note Book was out. On obtaining from the motorist an address in Kingussie the constable sternly addressed the hawker :—

" Now, then, you wi' the barra, what dae ye mean by backing into this gentleman's car ? "

At the time of the great Dunkirk evacuation a Skipper from Fraserburgh was on a visit with his wife to London.

During his stay word went round that anyone who could handle a vessel of any description was urgently requested to report at the South Coast port. He told his wife that he " had better jist gang " and would have to leave her alone for the day.

On arrival at the port, he was put in charge of a drifter and told to bring back as many of the British Army as he could from the Dunkirk beaches. On arrival at the other side he was confronted by tens of thousands of men. Even in the excitement of the great occasion, however, clannishness prevailed. Putting the megaphone to his mouth he shouted, " Onybody here frae Peterhe'd or the Broch ? "

The Sermon was being discussed and someone had suggested that there had been something in the address which the Minister had borrowed from Homer's Odyssey.

John, the Beadle, heard the remark, and as a loyal servant, immediately entered the lists in defence of his Minister.

" Nonsense," he stoutly replied. " You and your Homer ! It's mair likely Homer borrowed it frae oor man."

But the typical Scot is not merely content to uphold the prestige of his homeland. The spirit of loyalty demands that his own particular corner of it should be stubbornly defended before the world. Wander as he will, he clings tenaciously to the ties of his youth. The world is wide, but for every Scot there is a special centre round which it revolves.

A wounded Scottish soldier, recuperating in a London hospital, was asked where he had received his wounds. "Weel now," came the deliberate but characteristic reply, "it would be jist aboot twa mile on the Rothes side o' Baghdad!"

In the Border country this local patriotism is especially strong. Paris, he tells us, may have its points, but give him "Peebles for pleesure." Ask your devoted native of Moffat to marvel at the wonders of Niagara and he will stoutly affirm that they have wonders of their own at home—including "a peacock wi' a widden leg."

Go down to Hawick, and listen to the rabid local supporter at a Border Rugby Match.

One of the opposing team was playing a brilliant game; but the Teri supporter could hardly be expected openly to express admiration of the enemy.

Ultimately, however, he could contain himself no longer. "A graund player, that ane," he shouted to his neighbour, "a graund player—*his mither was a Hawick man.*"

Or move into Glasgow where the football loyalties are just as pronounced.

A well-known trainer to a prominent Scottish League Club had stuck faithfully to the Club for very many years, through good times and bad, although many tempting offers had been made for his services.

When his fame was at its height, he was being interviewed by an important English Club who were offering him very attractive terms to make a change. At last the visiting Chairman put the final question to the much sought after Scot.

"Now," he concluded, "these are the terms. But if there is anything else you want, we'll certainly try to meet you."

" Weel," came the reply, " it's a grand offer, and I think I'll accept—but on one condeetion."

" And what is the condition ? " smilingly asked the Chairman.

" The only condeetion," replied the faithful one firmly, " is that I get hame every Setterday tae support my ain team."

When the Scot finds himself ayont the Tweed he becomes more obstinately Scottish than ever. The smoke of his own country is more to him than any foreign fire. As Stevenson has it, " each new impression only deepens the sense of nationality and the desire of native places."

A native of Lyneside on his first visit to the South of England arrived when the nightingale was in song. Here, thought his English host, was an opportunity to treat his guest to a new experience—something he could never hear in his sterner North.

After listening to the melody for some time, and waiting in vain for some expression of pleasure from his visitor, the host asked with some impatience if the singing was not remarkably fine. " No bad, no bad," was the cautious reply, " but I wadna gie the wheeple o' a whaup for a' the nightingales that ever sang."

Talking of the Borders recalls other amusing instances of the effects of the excessive pre-occupation of the Scot with the affairs of his native town.

To celebrate the passing of the Reform Bill a great banquet was held in London. One of the Scottish representatives was a worthy provost from Tweedside, who, in the wining and dining, did full justice to the occasion.

In due course the main toast of the evening was proposed by a prominent member of the Government, when—to the surprise of his neighbours—the dutiful Scot was seen to rise, with becoming dignity, to respond. He was only induced to resume his seat when it was explained to him that the toast was " The Majesty of the People " and not " The Magistrates of Peebles."

A Borderer was on his first visit to London on a day excursion. Visiting a relation residing in the city he was informed that the streets seemed to be particularly crowded that day.

" Weel, weel," he replied, " ye must just expect that on a Hawick holiday."

Two stories of Sir Walter Scott's sturdy henchman, Tom Purdie, provide further illustrations of what is regarded as characteristically Scottish fidelity.

As a faithful servant he was overjoyed when the Baronetcy was conferred on his master. It was, however, with some concern that the faithful—if jealous—Tom heard of Sir Adam Ferguson's knighthood. With sterling and laudable *esprit de corps* he explained that " it might take the shine oot o' us."

Tom was, like most Tweedsiders, a keen fisher, and one morning he joined Sir Walter and an English guest just as the latter was in the act of taking a magnificent fish from the river. Tom, however, showed no inclination to share English elation, suggesting disparagingly that it would be " some sea brute." He was finally forced to admit, however, that it was as fine a trout as had been killed in Tweed for twenty years.

But Tom felt, in some vague irrational way, that by reason of the visitor's success, Sir Walter, the Borders, and Tweed had somehow been let down. As he passed the trout lying on the bank, he showed his resentment by giving it a violent kick in the head, exclaiming bitterly " To be ta'en by the like o' him frae London ! "

When it comes to incidents in his national history his patriotic zeal is even strong enough to shake him out of his native caution.

Witness the Bannockburn blacksmith who had shown some English visitors over the battlefield and who, for his services and his graphic descriptions of the events of that great day, had been offered half-a-crown. " Na, na, keep your money," he replied with great self-denial; "this affair has cost ye enough already."

Another noticeable characteristic of the Scot is his readiness to claim as a compatriot any one who has become a distinguished figure in any field of human endeavour. Did they not claim in Glasgow that the fanatical Robespierre was none other than a certain Rob Spier, a defaulting Solicitor who was taking a prolonged continental holiday? If not perhaps as marked as it was a generation ago, this " Wha's like us " attitude still persists. There is the familiar instance of the Officer of the London Scottish engaged in interviewing employers with a view to securing recruits for the Regiment.

" I am sorry," said one employer, " we have very few Scotsmen in our employment. I understand you want only Scots ? "

" Well," came the reply, " if we cannot get Scots, we are prepared to accept a few Superior English ! "

This in turn recalls the case of the young Soldier who, during the War, was asked how it had come about that he was the only Scotsman in an English Regiment. " Oh," he replied with a grin, " they've jist pit me in this lot to stiffen them up."

It is not surprising to learn that St. Peter himself is well aware of this outstanding characteristic and is not unsympathetic.

Hearing that a new applicant for admission to Paradise had arrived from Scotland, his greeting to the new arrival is reported to have been, " Well, you can come in—*but you're not going to like it* ! "

It cannot of course be denied that when his affections are engaged he does not ask himself too many questions.

When Dr Norman McLeod was minister of the Barony, one of the women in his congregation called in another clergyman in the neighbourhood to see her sick husband. Although he knew nothing of the household the stranger had willingly complied, but in the course of conversation asked whether the husband's family were not connected with some religious body in the city.

" Oh, aye," the wife replied, " we're a' members o' the Barony."

" Members of the Barony ? " exclaimed the visitor in surprise. " Then why didn't you call in Dr McLeod to pray with your husband instead of sending for me ? "

" Ca' in the great Dr Norman ! " cried the wife, " the man's surely daft. Dae ye no' ken this is a dangerous case o' typhoid fever ? "

But the persistent loyalty of the Scot is not always associated with places and persons. It will extend to local institutions, decried though they may be by the world outside.

In the early days of the West Coast Steamers, the highlander could not even accept the reproach that in the important matter of timekeeping there was room for some improvement. If the traveller complained of delays, and asked when the boat might be expected, he would get little satisfaction. Nothing suggesting anything in the nature of irregularity would be conceded.

One traveller in these old days had been waiting at Tobermory for some hours for the Skye boat. When at last it rounded the point and came into view, the intending traveller was alarmed to find that it was very much smaller than he had been led to expect. " Is *that* the Skye steamer ? " he exclaimed with concern to a native on the Pier, " *that thing* will never get to Skye ! " In a flash came the withering reply, " She'll be in Skye to-day—*if nothing happens to Skye*."

When he assumes his staunch defence of what he feels is his own he will make the very most of his case, however slender.

Dean Ramsay has recalled as an example of this trait the case of an old beadle from a North Country parish, who had been invited to spend some days in Glasgow with his old Minister now resident in the City.

Among other sights, the visitor was taken to the Cathedral. After showing him over all the great building, his host asked him what he thought of it all, after being accustomed to the Kirk at Mains.

" Weel Sir," said the beadle firmly, " you see she's bigger but she has nae laft—and she's sair fashed wi' thae pillars ! "

But perhaps a palm should go to Willie Pa'erson (twa T's), an old caddie at St. Andrews.

Some English visitors had arrived to find the Course shrouded in raw mist ; and, much to Willie's ill-concealed annoyance, there was a good deal of hand-blowing and arm-swinging to keep up the English circulation. Ultimately the complaints became vocal. " What weather ! What a climate ! " ventured one of the party, " Do you know it was beautiful weather in London when we left yesterday ? "

" Ach," replied Willie, with patriotic disgust, " nane o' your damned sunshine here ! "

Turn finally to Neil Munro for another choice example in " The Daft Days."*

Kate, the Dyce's maid, is in conversation with the newly-arrived visitor from America and has just been given specific information about the tremendous size of the continent.

" What a size ! " cried Kate, " Scotland's not slack for size neither ; there's Glasgow and Oban and Colonsay and Stornoway. There'll not be hills in America ? "

" There's no hills, just mountains," said Bud. " The chief mountain ranges are the Rocky Mountains and the Alleghanies. They're about the biggest mountains in the world."

" Talking about big things, look at the big pennyworth of milk we get here," said Kate, producing a can :

It was almost the last ditch of her national pride.

* Included by kind permission of William Blackwood & Sons Ltd.

PART TWO

SCOTTISH HUMOUR

SOME ADDITIONAL QUOTABLE EXAMPLES

STATUS

The Parish minister was on a visit of condolence to Mrs Scott, the widow of one of his congregation. A short church service having been arranged, the question of appropriate music arose. Had Mrs Scott any special preferences? No, she had no suggestions to make. Finally, the minister asked, " Well then, Mrs Scott, what about ' Now the labourers task is o'er?' "

" Oh! " cried Mrs Scott in alarm, " that'll no dae at a'! John was nane o' your labourers. He was a foreman at the Gasworks! "

A GENUINE GRIEVANCE

The Sermon had been on the doctrine of the Fall. We were, it seemed to Donald, doomed to suffering because one man had been weak enough to partake of the forbidden fruit. And Donald felt a real sense of grievance.

" It's gey hard on the likes o' me," he complained to his wife on the way home. " It comes very hard on me that never gied a damn for an aipple at ony time—*cookit or raw*."

GUID SCOTS BLOOD

Anyone coming in contact with the great numbers of tourists arriving in Scotland in yearly increasing numbers will have noticed that there are few among our visitors who are not at pains to claim that they have some Scots blood in their veins. Some of these proud claims have more substance than others.

In one very mixed party, details of lineages and family trees had been exchanged at length, when an African member of the party—black as a tinker's pot—put forward his unexpected but confident claim with the rest.

" You see," he explained, " my great, great grandfather was at the eating of a Scottish Missionary! "

UNFORTUNATE ACCIDENT

The night of the Bowling Club Supper had come and gone and the cronies were comparing notes about the success or otherwise of their journeys home from the feast.

" And how did you manage, Andra ? "

" Only middlin'," replied Andra. " The wife wadna have kent I was oot at a' if a great muckle Bobbie hadnae strampit on ma hand ! "

A WIFE AND HER SILLAR

As the old proverb has it, " a wife's aye welcome that comes wi' a crookit oxter." Tam—a North Country farmer—was of the same opinion and decided to marry a well-to-do widow in the district. It was not very long, however, before Tam began to see that she would not let him readily forget that he could do nothing much without *her* bawbees. Whenever he made a purchase of any kind she would nag at poor Tam and remind him that, but for her, he could not have put his hand in his pocket.

One day Tam brought home a horse from the market for his wife's inspection. After a pause she nodded and said, " Weel Tam, ye manna forget that if it hadna been for ma siller it wadna ha'e been here the day."

" Weel Meg," retorted the exasperated Tam, " if it hadna been for your siller ye wadna be here yersel ! "

PREMATURE CONGRATULATION

It was Burns' Nicht. John had celebrated not too wisely and got home in the wee sma' 'oors. At all costs his wife must never know.

Steadying himself, he got safely upstairs to find she was apparently fast asleep. He undressed—very quietly as he thought—and at last found himself happily in bed. But his smile of satisfaction vanished when his better half suddenly turned to make the severely practical remark :

" Man John, when you've done sae weel, it's a peety ye didnae take off your hat ! "

FULLY EXPLAINED

Andrew, the Laird's man, had received strict instructions in the morning that no visitors were to be allowed into the house that day. As luck would have it, the new Minister called in the course of the afternoon and was so obviously disappointed to learn that " the laird was oot," that Andrew thought the case was one calling for further explanation.

" Ye see, Sir," he assured the newcomer, " he's far frae weel. He's a *perfect martyr* tae the deleerium tremens ! "

FILIAL LOYALTY

The Minister had made a surprise Sunday afternoon call on one of his flock only to find he was not at home. Seeing his look of disappointment, the son of the house informed him that " he winna' be long—he's only away at the Golf Club."

The Minister's expression changed from one of disappointment to one of severe disapproval. Seeing his mistake, the youth hastened to re-assure him.

" Oh, he's no' playin' golf mind ye! No' on a Sunday! He's jist away for a wheen drinks and a game o' cairds."

THE MORNING AFTER

Morning worship at the Country Kirk had begun. The Parish Minister, taking the Service as usual, was famed throughout the countryside and beyond as a great student and lover of Burns. Indeed, at a local function on the previous night he had greatly added to his reputation by a striking speech in proposing " The Immortal Memory."

At the usual point in the Service, and with due gravity and sincerity, he called upon the congregation to join with him in what was known as the " long " prayer—a prayer traditionally containing appropriate expressions of adoration.

There were, however, few straight faces in the congregation when the worthy preacher, introducing the famous—in Scotland the household—words from " Tam o' Shanter," began :—

O, Lord, *Kings may be blest but Thou art glorious* !
O'er a' the ills o' life victorious.

MATERNAL PRIDE

Among the variety of learned pronouncements regarding the roots of laughter, there are many supporting the view that in all laughter there is a blend of mirth and sympathy : and it is probable that this familiar incident could be cited to illustrate what the sponsors of this theory have in mind.

The Highland Regiment had just been inspected, and, with bayonets flashing, were proudly marching down the crowded High Street to the stirring music of the pipes.

Suddenly, from an open window, a proud mother was heard to exclaim:

"They're a' oot o' step but oor Jock!"

FAITH—THEORY AND PRACTICE

A well-known Minister, whose name was familiar to all as the author of "Faith," was on a journey by ferry across a dangerous part of the sea loch. A sudden storm had blown up and the situation looked alarming.

He approached the Skipper anxiously and at last ventured to voice his fears and asked if there was any real danger.

"Och, keep your mind easy, Sir," said the Skipper quietly, "ye may be in Paradise in less than half-an-hoor."

"God forbid!" came the fervent reply.

DOUBTFUL "CHARACTER"

Hearing that very good wages were being paid to Trawler Deck hands, Erchie—a Newhaven joiner—went along to Leith to apply for a job. He was informed by the skipper that he could only take on men with good references as to character. As the disappointed joiner was turning away he saw with envy the next applicant accepted after producing what he heard the skipper to say was a first-rate certificate of honesty.

Before leaving the harbour, however, Erchie was recalled by the skipper and informed that, as a second man was wanted in a hurry, he would be taken on after all.

The ship had only been a day at sea when the new hand—with the testimonials—was given the job of doing some hammering at the head of the mast. Suddenly a heavy sea struck the ship and the workman—his tools with him—was swept overboard.

Meeting the skipper shortly afterwards Erchie stopped him to inquire:

"De ye mind that man you took on yesterday with the grand character?"

"Yes, yes, man," replied the skipper. "But what about it?"

"Weel," replied Erchie, with no trace of excitement, "he's awa' wi' your hammer!"

TRADING DIFFICULTIES

It is often difficult for the town dweller to appreciate the difficulties of crofters in remote parts of the country in obtaining certain of their household necessities.

One old Highlander had to face a twelve-mile walk for his provisions and had returned with a supply of matches. To his dismay he found that they would not light.

Back he went next day to complain to the village grocer. Anxious to show his customer that the matches were up to the usual standard, the merchant took one from a box, and drawing it across his trousers got it to light at the first attempt.

" You see, Donald," he said, " they're all right."

But Donald was not to be put off like this.

" And who," he asked, " is going to travel twelve miles to licht his matches on *your* breeks ? "

THE LAST WORD

The Minister was noted far beyond the bounds of his Parish for his scholarship and his skill in apt quotation, and one old member had brought a stranger with him to the morning service for what he promised would be a literary feast.

The expectant couple occupied a front pew and no sooner was the Sermon under way than the regular member began making audible remarks to his neighbour, identifying the sources of certain passages in the pulpit discourse.

" Imphm—that's a bit o' Shakespeare " he would announce. " Aye and that'll be frae Wordsworth " and so on. Interjections and commentary of this kind went on at regular intervals until at last the Minister's patience was exhausted.

Finally, in exasperation, he leaned over the pulpit and asked " if his brother in the front pew would be kind enough to keep his remarks to himself."

But the disturber was not to be so easily subdued.

" And that" he proudly explained to his fellow worshipper, " is a bit o' his ain."

THE NERVOUS SPEAKER

At the local Burns' Club supper Donald was called upon unexpectedly to propose a vote of thanks to the Chairman, a well-known farmer in the district.

After much stammering and chin-rubbing, Donald was at last able to propose his vote of thanks to the Chairman, adding that they must all be very pleased to see him " looking so much better efter being kicked in the face wi' a horse ! "

NOTABILITIES

A party comprising two English Bishops and two Cabinet Ministers had spent a fishing holiday in a remote hotel in Wester Ross. When the day of departure arrived the somewhat pompous and patronising spokesman for the quartet said to the worthy host :

" Well, John, I don't suppose you can have had four such distinguished visitors in your house before ! "

" Och ay, man, often," replied John, adding to the great delight of the other visitors within earshot, " only last week the blacksmith's four laddies were in—*and every one of them a piper.*"

PARENTAL ALARM

Old Donald, who had seldom been able to leave his croft, had at last accepted an invitation to spend a few days holiday in Edinburgh.

The special event of his stay was a visit to the Zoo where he displayed intense interest in all the exhibits. " This," he was told, " was a native of Africa ; that, again, was a native of India."

In due course it was the turn of the kangaroo to come under review. " And now," his guide informed Donald, " here is a native of Australia."

" Guid heavens ! " exclaimed Donald, with dismay, " ma dochter's mairrit tae one o' thae."

EXPLANATION FUTILE

Andra had had a good day in town but had imbibed rather too freely and the upshot was that he lost the last train home.

Going to the nearest Post Office he asked the counter girl to write a telegram to his wife saying, " missed train." The assistant, sympathetic, and anxious to assist one in obvious trouble, suggested that he could add a few more words without further cost, explaining *how* he had missed it.

Steadying himself for a moment, Andra replied, " Never mind, lassie, *she'll* ken ! "

IDENTIFIED

Mrs McKay, in all her city finery, had returned to the village after some years absence to visit her husband's grave. She was, however, having difficulty in tracing the actual position in the cemetery and with an assumed " lone-widow " air had approached Erchie, the new gravedigger, for some assistance. In reply to Erchie's preliminary enquiries she informed him that the name was McKay.

" I'll need mair particulars," returned Erchie. " Losh woman, there are dizzens o' MacKays lying here."

" He was a Thomas MacKay," went on the widow. " Poor Thomas, he was a worthy man, but very, very strict. He always said that if I was ever unfaithful to his memory he would turn in his grave."

" I have ye noo," cried Erchie. " I've got ye, ye'll mean ' Birling Tam ',"

LOVE'S LABOUR LOST

An Edinburgh school teacher's day was considerably brightened by receiving one morning the following note from a pupil's mother :—

" Please do not blame Willie for not doing the sum about walking from Edinburgh to Glasgow. It would take too long.

" The last time you asked about how long it would take to walk five times from the Castle to Holyrood, his father lost a morning's work. And after all his walking you went and marked the sum wrong."

DIFFICULTIES OF A STUDENT

The Evening School classes in a town in the West were attended for the most part by workers in the adjoining ship-yards. As the students had been showing commendable zeal in their desire to overcome certain deficiences in their earlier education, a Professor of English was invited to visit the class in his subject with the object of adding a further stimulus to their efforts at self-improvement.

No sooner had the Professor entered the classroom than a voice from the back benches was heard to exclaim : " Hey, Sir ! A've nae pencil ! "

Seizing the opportunity to introduce a touch of learning, the Professor addressed the class in general and the interrupter in particular :—

> " I have no pencil
> Thou hast no pencil
> He has no pencil
> We have no pencils
> You have no pencils
> They have no pencils."

" Weel," came the aggrieved voice again, " whae's *got* a' the bloomin' pencils ? "

FOOTBALL RELIGION

It was New Year's Day at Ibrox Park, Glasgow, and the crowd were awaiting the appearance of the players.

When the Rangers turned out, a rabid supporter in the stand noisily voiced his enthusiasm, waving a light-blue hat with great vigour. His immediate neighbour sat silent and unimpressed. When the Celtic team appeared, the spectator on the other side of the silent one also rose and lustily shouted his welcome to his favourites—again to the accompaniment of much waving of a green tam-o'-shanter.

Realising, in the hush before the whistle, that no sign had come from his neighbour and that apparently he supported *neither* team, the supporter of the " Blues " was heard to exclaim in disgust, " He must be yin o' thae damned atheists."

SEQUEL

The sequel to the above story relates that the Celtic team suffered defeat.

As he left the grandstand the depressed Celtic supporter was heard to lament :

" Man, man, this is an awfu' business ! There'll be mony a sad he'rt in the Vatican this nicht."

FINAL EXCUSE

Young Alec had not been long in his job as office boy before he found it necessary to ask the Manager if he could have the afternoon off to attend his grandmother's funeral.

"Why, yes," replied the Manager kindly. "I can quite understand that you will want to be at the final scene."

"Thank you very much, Sir," said Alec, greatly relieved. "But it's no the final—it's only the semi-final."

PARTING SHOT

Jock was a regular attender at all football matches at one of the larger Glasgow grounds, not so much to support the home team as to give expression to his disgust at the display of one of the backs of the ground club, of whose standard of play Jock had a very poor opinion indeed.

"Look at him!" he would shout. "Jist look at him! He couldna kick a hole in a wet newspaper!"

This flow of abuse would go steadily on until, towards the close of one game, the victim, in a desperate clearance, drove the wet and heavy ball hard into the terracing hitting Jock full in the face.

There was silence for a moment from the badly shaken Jock. But, replacing his cap, he soon resumed his vocal exercises.

"Weel," he shouted, "A'll say this for ye, *you're no deef!*"

GOLF: THE PURIST

When golf techniques and scores are discussed there are some who maintain that "how" it is done is less important than "in how few." But they will have none of this doctrine in the East Neuk of Fife.

On her first visit to St. Andrews, a young girl decided to have her first lesson from one of the local instructors and in fear and trembling she made her way to the practice ground for the appointed ordeal. Instead of beginning with driver practice, the method adopted by her tutor was to place a mashie in the pupil's hands with instructions to play for a hole some 50 or 60 yards away.

Almost too nervous to hold the club, our young pupil finally summoned up courage enough to hit the ball towards the prescribed target, and, to her surprise and delight, the ball finished in the hole. She turned to her instructor for some sign of approval. But with his critical eye on her grip and stance all she got was a sad shake of his head and the severe reply of the purist:

"Naw, Naw. That'll no dae at a'. You're daein' it a' wrang!"

SUPER OPTIMISM

In the early rounds of the Scottish Cup Competition, it is frequently the luck of the draw that one of the small Country Clubs meets one of the leading First Division League Clubs.

In a first round tie some years ago the Vale of Atholl were drawn to meet Rangers at Ibrox Park, Glasgow, and the occasion was naturally one of great moment for the natives of Dunkeld and district. For the benefit of those unable to make the trip to Glasgow, it was arranged that the final score would be telegraphed to the local Post Office.

In due course the telegram arrived and the local Postmaster put his head round the door to make the bare announcement, " Score 15-0," to the waiting crowd.

There was a stunned silence among the local supporters of the " Vale," till one brave voice was raised to ask, " *Whae for* ? "

CRASS IGNORANCE

Prior to the commencement of one of the International matches at Tynecastle Park, Edinburgh, the discussion among the spectators was, as is usual on such occasions, concerned with the football personalities of a former day.

One rabid Hearts' supporter was loudly declaring that " Bobbie Walker " was the finest player of all time. An English excursionist nearby replied that he had never heard the name in his life before.

" Never heard o' Bobbie Walker ! " came the incredulous reply. " Away, man, and read your Bible."

SAGE ADVICE

The eminent scholar was speaking of his experiences as an impecunious student and declaring how much he had profited from one particular bit of advice he had received from his worthy landlady.

" Now, John ", she often told him, " never forget this ! if ever ye want onything, dinna forget tae tell me—and I'll tell ye hoo tae dae withoot it ! "

WORLDLY WEALTH

The Minister had been asked by the village cobbler if he would witness his will and say whether he approved his many bequests.

" Well, John, " replied the Minister, if you care to confide in me, I'll advise you if I can."

" Weel," John began, " I've willed a thoosand tae my hoosekeeper, and a thoosand tae each o' my twa brithers. Tae my apprentice—a guid daein' lad—I'm leavin' five hunner, and . . . "

" But John," interrupted the Minister, in surprise, " I had no idea you had so much money."

"Money ? " replied the equally surprised cobbler. " That's no money. That's tackets! "

A BUBBLE BURST

The village grocer had ambitions. Like many another before him, he had " a lurking wish to appear considerable in his native place ". He meant to climb, and he saw that the one certain way of raising his social status and prestige was to secure election to the County Council.

Before actually proceeding, he thought he would ascertain how the land lay, and asked his vanman to mention casually to some of the more influential of his customers that he was contemplating County Council work, and let him know the result. When the vanman returned, the grocer asked him anxiously if he had done as he had suggested " aboot yon."

" Oh, aye " replied the vanman, " I tell't them at a' the big hooses."

" And what did they say ? " enquired the grocer eagerly.

" Oh, naething," came the reply. " They jist laughed! "

UNSOLICITED TESTIMONIAL

John was a Fifer, and a golfer, and a good one at that. But he never lost an opportunity of impressing upon others the excellence of his own play.

He was playing an important tie and the game had reached the turn. He was being passed on an adjoining fairway by a local rival who crossed over to hear what John had to contend with.

" What kind o' a player are you up against to-day John ? "
he asked.

" O he's a great player *this*," replied John at once.

" What like's his driving," continued the inquirer.

" Doon the middle every time," John assured him, " and
nearly oot o' sicht."

" What aboot his irons then ? " came the next question.

" Deid on the pin every time," was the reply, " he's deadly
richt enough.   Never a mistake ! "

" Weel then," said the other, after receiving similar glowing
accounts of the short game, but looking for some flaw in the
play of this paragon, " he'll be weak on the greens ? "

" No him ! " John countered at once, " he strokes them in
frae all angles.   What a player !   What a putter ! "

With such an account of his opponent's play it only remained
for John's rival to raise the delicate question of the state of the
game.

" And hoo many are ye doon then, John ? " came the final
question with a touch of satisfaction in the smile.

" Doon ? " exclaimed John as he moved away, " I'm no
doon at a'.   I'm twa up ! "

GOLFER'S MODESTY

When golfers meet for the first time during the holiday
season, there is a good deal of " approach " work to be done
before handicaps can be satisfactorily arranged.   Each tries to
outdo the other in understating the standard of his own play.
An incident of this kind was being recounted in his home
clubhouse by a member returning from a St. Andrews holiday.

" Ay," the member was explaining, " I asked him what
like handicap he had.   He said he was a puir 18 man and swore
to me he hadna' played for six month.   Weel, says I, I havena
handled a club for a twelve month and am bad wi' the lumbago.

" We said we'd play for half-a-croon.   And believe me or
believe me no, I had to dae twa under fours tae beat him ! "

THE BENEFIT OF THE DOUBT

Andra, one of the old school, had been employed as a caddie
for a full month by a distinguished visitor to the Fife coast.
Anxious to improve his game during his stay, the visitor had
announced that if and when he " broke " 100, Andra was to
have a bottle of whisky to mark the occasion.

Despite the player's efforts and all that Andra could do by
way of advice and encouragement, the final round on the final

day had arrived with the 100 still unbroken. Play proceeded in a tense atmosphere until, standing on the 18th tee, a moderate 5 was all that was required to achieve the elusive 99—and the equally elusive bottle.

To Andra's dismay however, the over-anxious player was short of the green in 3. The critical moment had come ; but it was too much for the nervous visitor, and his 98th stroke finished 15 yards beyond the hole.

But Andra was equal to the occasion. Rushing forward to pick up the ball he shouted excitedly, " Weel done, Sir ! Ye've done it. Onybody would gie ye that yin."

SHARP PRACTICE

The English visitor to the Ross-shire moors had been assuring the company that he had a very high reputation as a crack shot. So confident was he in his powers that he promised that for every bird he missed he would give a shilling to Donald, his ghillie.

Telling the story to his cronies at night, Donald added, " Aye, it was a guid day's sport ! Anither blank cartridge an' I'd have had a pound ! "

BAD SHOOTING

During the war the work of the Home Guard sometimes had its amusing moments.

In one of the outlying Districts the volunteers were for the most part miners, many of whom had never before handled a gun.

A new recruit arrived for his first night at target practice.

He fired half a dozen shots at a 100 yards and was wide with every shot. He was given another half-dozen attempts but was wider than ever.

At last he stood up, threw down his rifle in disgust, and convulsed the Company by demanding " For guidness sake, gie's a stane ! "

MIXED SHOOTING

A Highland Proprietor before going abroad had advertised his shootings as " to let " and had instructed his gamekeeper to give the shooting a favourable reputation when inquiries were received from any prospective tenants.

The first inquirer was an English sportsman and he naturally asked how the place was stocked. " Were there any deer ? "

" Oh ay," replied the Keeper, " thoosands o' them."

A little bit suspicious, the visitor again inquired, " And I suppose there are plenty of grouse ? "

" Deed aye," came the ready assurance, " thoosands o' them as well."

" And pheasants ? "

" Yes indeed—thoosands o' pheasants."

Thinking it time to put a stop to these wild estimates, the English visitor asked if there were any gorillas.

" Weel," came the more cautious reply, " they are no *just* sae plentiful. They come just whiles, ye ken, like your honour's self."

PRESTIGE

A famous Chancellor of the Exchequer was obtaining a brief respite from the cares of office by spending a short golfing holiday at St. Andrews. Wherever he went he was, of course, recognised as the great Statesman, the impressive World figure. But the young Fifer who caddied for the celebrity had different ideas.

At the end of the day's golf he quietly announced " Man, sir ! Wi' your height and ma brains, we'd mak' a gran' pair in a foursome ! "

It was no doubt the same young realist who solemnly informed the University Professor that " onybody can teach Greek but gowf needs a heid ! "

BUSINESS PROSPECTS

The local poacher was making one of his periodic appearances in a Border Court. He was, as usual, found guilty and a fine of forty shillings was imposed with the option of ten days imprisonment.

Again, as usual, he pled his inability to pay and the Sheriff asked him how long it would take him to raise the money.

" Weel, my Lord," replied the accused with a bland look of innocence, " it's hard to say. It a' depends on hoo the fish come up the water."

A slight variant of the foregoing example concerns another poacher faced with the same alternative, and asking for time to pay.

" And why do you need time to meet the fine imposed ? " asked the Sheriff.

" It's this way, ma lord," he complained, " money's gey hard to come by when folk grudge half a croon for a hare."

UNIQUE DISTINCTION

The widow of a village worthy was approached by her minister and asked if there was anything she would like him to mention specially at the funeral service—something for which the deceased was likely to be remembered.

Like many of her kind the widow had her own definite if unconventional point of view.

" Well, sir," she replied, after some reflection, " there's one thing. Wad ye jist say that he was the only man in the parish that could dance the Heilan' Fling on a peat ! "

LANGUAGE DIFFICULTIES

A foreign visitor to Scotland had just returned from a bus tour. He had greatly enjoyed the scenery and the company, and he wanted more.

Calling at the bus office, he asked if he could book for the places his recent companions were due to visit next week. Could he have a ticket for Auld Claes and Parritch on Monday?

COLD RECEPTION

Old Mrs MacKay was a woman with a grievance. She was, she firmly believed, being neglected by her minister, who, having deputed his work of visitation to his assistant, had not called on her for over a year.

The minister was a great student of Botany and was famous far beyond the bounds of his Parish for his published works and his collection of rare specimens.

After three visits by the assistant, the minister did at last present himself in person at Mrs MacKay's door. There was a flinty look in her eye as she greeted him :—

" Oh, it's you, is't ? Weel, a' I'll say is this. If I had been some kind o' fancy puddock stool, ye'd ha' been here long afore noo."

INVOLUNTARY CONTRIBUTOR

In the same village you would also be told about the down-at-heel tramp coming out of the Manse gate who met another on the road in.

" Ye neednae waste yer time in there," he said to the new-comer. " He's just got a shillin' oot o' me for the foreign missions."

A BAD CASE OF *LOCUM TENENS*

Old Mrs Macintyre was on her annual visit to Glasgow to her daughter who was naturally anxious to get all the news of the activities and personalities of her native village.

The daughter had always shown an affectionate interest in the welfare of the folk at the manse, and ultimately asked how her old minister was now faring.

" Oh," she was informed, " he's been badly for the last six months, puir man."

" Dear, dear, mother, that's a long time to be off," replied the daughter. " Has he got a *locum tenens* ? "

" Na, na," replied the mother, " naething like that—just the same auld pain in his back."

FAINT PRAISE

The village pulpit had been occupied for several weeks by an eminent D.D. from the city. After taking his final service, the Doctor was in conversation with two of the elders, and— anxious to obtain a parting word of approval—ventured to mention that no one in the congregation had as yet said whether his sermons had been appreciated.

The first elder responded without hesitation.

" Weel," he volunteered, " I must say I've heard worse ! "

The reverend Doctor turned hopefully to the second elder. He was equally ready with his encouragement.

" Pay nae attention to him, Doctor, he *often* gets cairried away ! "

THE FAME OF JOHN WHITE

A minister from the far North was on a visit to Edinburgh and had boarded a busy tram at the Waverley Station bound for Gorgie Road. He was no sooner seated than he saw a headline in his neighbour's newspaper : " £8,000 *for John White*," referring to the transfer fee of the then popular centre-forward of the Heart of Midlothian Football Club.

The reverend gentleman not unnaturally assumed that this announcement concerned a further handsome addition to Dr John White's Church Extension Fund, a cause which he and his own congregation had very much at heart. He could not resist the impulse to express his pleasure to his fellow-passenger.

" Man," he said to him, " that's grand news you have in your paper. £8,000 is a lot of money."

" Oh aye," replied his neighbour, more interested in football personalities than Church Extension Funds, " it's a big sum right enough. But, ye ken, John White's a guid man."

" Your right there, my friend," replied the minister, " White always has a goal in view and goes straight for it, in face of all obstacles."

" Ay," agreed the football follower, " he goes for the goal a' richt."

The minister nodded assent, and after a moment's pause, volunteered the information that he knew White's brother Willie. As it happened both the famous Johns had " Willies " as brothers each of whom was well-known in the Church and the world of sport respectively.

" I ken Willie White mysel," replied the sportsman, thinking of the Heart's goalkeeper.

" Yes," continued the minister, " a fine man Willie—although not so well-known as his brother."

" No, man," continued the man from Gorgie with his own line of thought, " ye never read sae much aboot Willie. But of course he'll never be the man his brother John is."

In the ensuing exchanges the minister loyally continued his defence of the less eminent but the other would have none of it. He rose to leave the tram.

" I dinna care what ye say," was his parting shot, " Willie's no in the same street as John."

But the minister had the last word.

" Not in the same *street* ? " he shouted to the retreating figure, " man he's not even in the same Presbytery ! "

SATISFACTION GUARANTEED

The minister only discovered when in the pulpit that he had mislaid his morning sermon. As there were some visitors in church he thought it best to explain his predicament.

"My friends," he announced, "I may as weel tell ye that I've mislaid the notes for my sermon to-day, so I must ask you to bear with me as I can only pass on whatever words the Lord puts into my mouth. But if you can manage to come to the Evening Service I can assure you you'll hear something worth listening to."

PRIDE OF AN EXILE

The young domestic had been in London for a long time before her mistress discovered she came from Aberdeen.

"Why didn't you mention this before, Annie?" she asked.

"Well" came the prompt reply, "it was jist that I didna like tae boast!"

PRACTICAL SOLUTION

Young John was noted in the village and beyond as a staunch and rabid tee-totaller. To the genuine surprise of his parents—who were equally strict where "drink" was concerned —he had announced his engagement to marry a young lady who had but recently succeeded to a thriving public house.

But young John faced a problem. He explained to his father that he would require to live in the business premises and had been greatly disturbed to learn that he would be expected as "mine host" to join his customers in an occasional friendly drink. Here was a dilemma—and what did his father think?

John senior nodded slowly and promised to give the problem careful thought. The next day he announced that he had seen the light.

"Weel John," he said, "your mither and me can see what a sore temptation it will be with so much drink aboot. But we ken fine that business is aye business and we see nae harm in your having a bit drink whiles wi' the customers—as long as you dinna enjoy it!"

ORDER OF PRECEDENCE

The scene was a West Highland Pier and the afternoon boat was being tied up.

" Anything important to-day Skipper ? " shouted the Piermaster.

" Nothing at all," replied the Skipper, " nothing much at all, only two bulls and a Meenister ! "

SCOTS CAUTION

Two shipwrecked Scots had been hanging on for hours to an upturned boat. Jock, realising that he might not be able to hold out much longer, began to recount his past misdeeds, and to vow that if he escaped he would in future lead an entirely new life. Suddenly, there was a cry from his comrade in distress:

" Haud on, Jock! Dinna commit yersel'—A think A see land! "

NORTHERN AUSTERITY

At the morning service in a Presbyterian Kirk in the North, a visitor from the South had made his appearance. It was soon evident that he was accustomed to a less severe atmosphere during Divine Worship, and from time to time disturbed the normal calm by exclaiming " Hallelujah! Hallelujah! Praise the Lord ! "

This went on for some time, until an old elder moved forward to the interrupter, tapped him on the shoulder and warned him—

" Look here, ma man, *we dinna praise the Lord here* ! "

A TEXT FROM BURNS

Returning one quiet summer evening to his Manse the Minister stopped at a cottage door to have a chat with one of his flock.

They talked easily enough about mutual interests for a short time as they gazed on the quiet Border hills, but gradually the flow of conversation ceased.

At last the Minister broke one of the long silences by murmuring as he pointed to the landscape, " I to the hills will lift mine eyes."

" Aye man," replied the other, finding himself as he thought on safe ground. " Aye, Rabbie Burns was the boy ! "

THE LAST STRAW

John was tenant of a small farm in the North. One of the old school, he was a hard worker and fiercely impatient of any set-backs. Bad weather for weeks on end, had, however, badly disorganized work on the farm and in particular there had been serious delay in getting in his hay. He was, however, relying on the promise of assistance from a relative who was Chief Officer on the *Queen Elizabeth* and residing in the district on leave.

At last the weather improved and work was to commence next day. The Chief Officer duly appeared at the farm as arranged but only to report that he had been suddenly recalled to his ship which was due to sail that night.

All his plans thus upset, John was at first speechless with anger.

" Dammit ! Dammit ! " he stormed. " Can the *Queen Elizabeth* no wait and sail on a wet day ! "

GOOD SHOOTING

All Highlanders pride themselves that their particular part of the country provides the very best sport; and they will not admit that any other district can possibly have game in equal variety.

At the commencement of the shooting season, a sportsman from the South asked one of the local patriots whether there were any centenarians on the island.

This was a new one for the native; but at all costs he must uphold the reputation of his moors.

" Weel, now," he replied cautiously, " I am not just too sure about that. Indeed, I heard a story at the Post Office that the very last one was shot only yesterday. "

" A SMACK O' THE GRUESOME "

A criticism often levelled against the earlier examples of the humour of Scotland was that it unduly emphasized the note of grimness and the macabre. There was perhaps some ground for the charge and these few examples may be enough by way of illustration.

The scene is, of course, the village Kirkyaird and the gravedigger is displaying to a villager a large human bone unearthed in the course of his work.

" Wha's dae ye think it is ? " asked the spectator.

" It looks like a Fraser's," replied the digger at once. After a pause for closer inspection he went on : " Ay it's a Fraser richt enough. It's Meg Fraser's hench bane." A further pause for reflection and he added with admiration. " They didna bring up thae kind on cookies ! "

A CLEAR CONSCIENCE

Old John was unburdening himself after his wife's funeral.

" Ay," he was heard to say, " a' I can say is that I've been guid tae her. A gey auld Kist she brocht when she cam—and look what she's awa' in ! "

A GUID CONCEIT

Andrew had " a guid conceit o' himsel' " as a vocalist; but even his best friends knew that his appearances on local programmes would have been few indeed but for the fact that no other singer was available in the town.

The day came, however, when an ambitious musical event was arranged, the special attraction being the appearance of a celebrated vocalist with a European reputation. Here, said the knowing ones, was a unique opportunity to let Andrew hear first-class singing.

After the concert Andrew was asked for his impressions.

" Well, now, " came the confident reply; " A've come tae the conclusion that the only difference between him and me is *praactice*! "

RURAL HARMONY

The English visitor was making his visit to a village in the north and was hearing from the neighbours about the activities of those fortunate enough to live among the beauties of the bens and glens. Everything about the place suggested rural peace and harmony until he received the revealing reply to his final question.

"And how many churches have you here ? " he asked.

" Weel," came the final reply, " there were two—but we had an amalgamation—and noo there's *three*."

TEMPTATION

A rather battered parcel addressed to the local minister had arrived at the village Post Office. Through the openings in the torn wrapping it could be easily seen that a supply of Bibles was in transit. Noting the expensive bindings and the beautiful gilt pages the postie thought it would be advisable to hand over his precious charge to the minister personally.

When handing over his parcel later in the day he remarked to the minister with some severity :

" Fancy sending good Bibles in sic a like parcel. Onybody a bit religious might help himself to yin or twa."

THE CHURCH AND THE LAW

A prominent figure in the legal world has recalled a conversation of his student days with a North Country farmer who was interested enough to ask if he was studying for the ministry.

" Oh, no," replied the student, " I'm not going to be a minister—I'm going to be a lawyer."

" Man, man," said the farmer, with a slow shake of the head, " *Jist the opposite* ! "

PRESCRIPTION FOR LONGEVITY

The old couple, still hale and hearty, were celebrating their diamond wedding, and to mark the occasion had received a special call from the Parish Minister.

As the visitor was about to leave, he asked if they could name their own special secret to account for their longevity.

" Oh, ay," answered John readily enough, " it's mairriage ! "

The minister beamed with pleasure. He could hardly wait to hear the further story of domestic harmony over the years.

" Marriage for long life, John," he replied, " now that's most interesting . . . I . . ."

But John cut him short.

" Ye see," he went on, " this is the way o't. After I was mairried I said to the wife, ' Meg,' I says, ' I maun warn ye that I've a gey sherp tongue in my heid, and I'm thinking that whiles ye'll hear the edge o't. But when ye've had as much as ye can stand, ye can aye open the door and gang oot for a walk ! '

' Weel, John,' says Meg—nippy like—' ye'll learn quick enough that I've a gey sherp tongue mysel' ! And when things get ower hot for *you*—weel, as ye say yersel', there's aye the open door and a bit walk ! '

"Ay, ay," concluded John with a wry smile, " that's oor secret—plenty o' exercise and fresh air ! "

A QUESTION OF DAMAGES

After much persuasion Donald had been induced to make his first railway journey to Edinburgh. As the train neared its destination a serious collision occurred and ultimately poor Donald found himself lying among a mass of wreckage.

With great difficulty he was finally rescued by a brother Scot, who, in an attempt to reassure the victim, reminded him that there would, of course, be the question of damages.

" Damages ! " returned the aggrieved Donald. " Damages ? It wasna' me that cowpit yer train ! "

DEFAMATION OF CHARACTER

During the hearing of a case in the Licensing Court the witness had been rather verbose and vague in his replies during his examination.

" Keep a little more to the point if you can," finally suggested the Agent : " You are, I am afraid, a little ambiguous."

" That's a *lie*," came the heated reply, " I've been on the teetotal for three month ! "

LOGIC FROM THE DOCK

A small town worthy, on his appearance in Court, was asked whether he pleaded guilty or not guilty to a charge of being " drunk and disorderly."

" Hoo am I tae ken, your Worship ? " he complained, " till I hear the evidence ? I was blin' fu' at the time ! "

THE NERVOUS MAGISTRATE

The Case before the newly appointed Magistrate concerned the theft of a pig. In an endeavour to overcome his nervousness, he contrived his most stern demeanour and gravely declared to the accused that pig-stealing was now far too prevalent in the burgh, and that " unless an example was made in this case, *none of us will be safe.*"

STORAGE DIFFICULTIES

A party of motorists had stopped at a remote farm house for some milk. When this had been duly supplied, one of the party said to the farmer how much they admired the lovely view from the house and how much they envied anyone living in such a beautiful place.

" That's a' verra weel," returned the farmer, " but hoo wad you like to travel fifteen mile every time ye wanted a bit gless o' whiskey ? "

" Oh, well," replied the tourist, " surely you could get half a dozen bottles and keep it in the house."

But the farmer shook his head.

" It'll no dae," he replied sadly, " whisky winna keep ! "

RETORT DISCOURTEOUS

In his days as an advocate Lord Cockburn unsuccessfully defended in a murder case in which the evidence against the accused seemed to be conclusive. The death sentence was pronounced and the date of execution fixed for some weeks ahead.

As Cockburn was passing the condemned man the latter protested that he had not got justice that day.

" Maybe no'," was the reply of the realist Cockburn " maybe no'—but you'll get it on the 3rd o' March."

DISCIPLINARY ACTION

After a medical examination of a class of school children the teacher found it necessary to send a note to one of the parents intimating that "your son Thomas shows signs of Astigmatism and this should be attended to."

On the following day the teacher received a reply from the mother saying : " I dinna ken what it is that Tommy has been daein' ; but I leathered him last night and again this mornin'—and that oucht tae dae some guid ! "

MATERNAL DISAPPOINTMENT

Auld Mrs McIntyre, hearing that certain advantages in matters of food and clothing were enjoyed by children at a certain school reserved for pupils somewhat below the normal level of intelligence, had made up her mind that it would solve some of her own problems if her wee Aggie could obtain admission.

One day, however, her neighbours were surprised to see Mrs McIntyre and her Aggie returning home in the forenoon—both weeping copiously. "What's wrang, what's wrang," anxiously enquired the neighbours. Mrs McIntyre, stemming the tide of her tears for a moment, replied :

" Wee Aggie's been examined for the daft Schule—and *she's failed* ! "

THE BITER BIT

It was the custom some years ago in some parts of Scotland for some of the older farm lads to return to school during the quiet season to make up in some measure for broken time at other periods of the year.

They were naturally rather difficult to handle, and the records tell of the experience of an elderly little schoolmaster who made up his mind to enforce discipline by applying the tawse at every possible opportunity.

One of the bigger lads was one day brought out for punishment, and he dutifully held out his hand which was about as big as a ham. The poor old schoolmaster laid on the tawse for all he was worth, but, after great puffing and blowing, made little or no impression on the offender. Finally, he stopped his applications, completely exhausted.

" Aye, my mannie," said the youth, quite unperturbed, " that'll gaur ye swyte."

STRICTLY CORRECT

A good-natured old Scots farmer entered a tramcar one afternoon and found himself seated beside a small boy returning from school.

" And do you like the skule, my mannie ? " asked the farmer.

" Aye," said the boy, bashfully.

" That's grand," continued the farmer, " and I'm sure you'll be a guid scholar. But how do ye stand in your class ? "

" Second dux," promptly replied the boy.

" Second dux ! did you say ? Weel you deserve something for that," and he thrust sixpence into the boy's hand.

" And hoo many's in your class ? " continued the farmer.

" Me and a wee lassie," came the unabashed reply.

A FLOWING TONGUE

A few cronies were discussing the merits of their respective ministers. One had claimed that his man had been known to preach six different sermons from the same text. A second went further and claimed that his minister could preach twelve sermons in as many weeks from the shortest text in the Bible.

Andrew, who during the argument had been silent in the corner, at last removed his pipe from his mouth to say :

" Man, that's naething ! Naething ! My wife's been preaching at me for the last forty year frae nae text at a'."

THE VOICE OF AUTHORITY

The atmosphere in the Council chamber was tense. Throughout the sitting there had been prolonged and fiery exchanges between the Provost and the Senior Bailie. The Authority of the Chair was being repeatedly challenged by the loquacious Bailie, and tempers were rising.

At last the Provost could stand no more. Pointing to the offender he thundered :

" See here, Bailie Broon. What we want frae you is Silence ! *And damned little o' that* ! "

FAIR WARNING

An old worthy on the Leuchars side of St. Andrews was having trouble with his hens. They would persist in wandering on the nearby branch line and his losses had been heavy.

At last, in desperation, he obtained a Railway poster giving a full list of the local trains. This he carefully nailed to the hen-house door, muttering to himself as he left, "Weel, if ye get run ower noo, it's your ain damned fau't."

LOGIC

The County Schoolmaster had made it a practice to encourage parents to consult him, at the close of each year, before deciding on the careers of the children then leaving school.

Mrs MacFarlane duly presented herself with her young Willie, but made it clear at once that she had her own decided views on the subject.

" I've just come to tell ye," she announced, " that Willie's to be a butcher."

" A butcher ? " exclaimed the disappointed master. " A butcher ? Why on earth do you want him to be a butcher ? "

" Weel," she replied, " his he'rts fair set on it. He's that fond o' animals ! "

DISCOVERY

A University Research party was engaged in compiling information regarding living conditions and kindred topics affecting the smaller islands in the Hebrides and one day sighted a small island which promised to be a suitable place to pursue their enquiries.

Helped ashore by a lone figure on the rough jetty, they lost no time in commencing their cross-examination.

" And how many people actually live here ? " was the first question.

" Well, now," replied the islander, "there's me, and the wife, and the wife's sister—just the three of us."

The visitors shewed increased interest.

" And now," they went on, " what kind of place is this to live in ? "

" Oh ! " came the prompt reply, " a terrible place for scandal ! "

THE HIGHLANDER AGAIN

Donald was famed throughout one of the islands in the West as a man of very many parts. He was a geologist. He was a botanist. He wrote poems and recited them. He composed songs and sang them. He made harps and fiddles and was an exponent of both. There was little he could not do.

A distinguished visitor to the island, hearing of this local prodigy, expressed a wish to meet him. In due course a meeting was arranged, and the visitor was not long in coming to the conclusion that he had indeed met a very remarkable man.

As he was taking his leave, the visitor assured Donald that he greatly admired and, indeed, envied his varied accomplishments.

Donald merely nodded and smiled. After a pause, however, he spoke :

" Och, well, it's jist as you say." A further pause, and he added, " Man, if I had the ingredients I could make *thunder*."

AND HIS WIFE

Not only the Highlander himself but his wife also will show from time to time that she considers herself to be of some importance in the scheme of things. She can make it clear that she regards her particular opinions and judgments of sufficient moment to cause some concern to those in high places.

An example of this turn of mind is recorded by a certain Bishop who had occasion, during a Highland tour, to spend a night in a cottage in Applecross. To the Bishop's surprise, the gudewife displayed quite a remarkable knowledge of current affairs and, in the course of fireside exchanges, the merits and demerits of the then Archbishop of Canterbury came under review. She was at some pains to inform her visitor that she could not approve anything the Archbishop said, or thought, or did, and she hoped that the Bishop would convey her views to the proper quarter !

As the Bishop was leaving the following morning, the gudewife let him have her parting reminder :

" Noo mind and tell yon Archbishop o' yours that there's an auld wife in Applecross keepin' her eye on him ! "

TAKING HIM DOWN

It was not often that old Mrs Mearns went very far from her native North. One day, however, she found herself at the Railway Station having some trouble with a bumptious and impatient young booking clerk. To her most reasonable, if anxious, inquiries about her journey, all she could obtain by way of reply was a curt and sometimes impertinent " Ask a porter."

But Mrs Mearns was determined to get satisfaction ; and as the exchanges between the two grew hotter a crowd had gathered round her, which led the official to become even more aggressively brusque and objectionable.

Finally Mrs Mearns was thoroughly roused.

" Noo, ma mannie," she asked, " div ye ken fa ye mind me o' ? "

" No, I do *not*," snapped the enemy.

" Weel, then," comes the reply, to the great delight of the now considerable crowd, " ye jist mind me o' the mannie that cam tae sweep ma grannie's lum, and stack i' the middle o't. *He was ower big for the place he was in.*"

INTER-CITY RIVALRY

Everybody in Scotland is familiar with the keen, but more or less friendly, rivalry which has always existed between Edinburgh and Glasgow.

Neil Munro used to say that there was nothing wrong with Edinburgh—as long as you had a book to read when you were in it. But even if, over the years, Glasgow folk seem to have had the better of the exchanges, Edinburgh can from time to time respond with a sharp thrust.

The alleged occasion was a public competition organised to advertise a Suburban Shopping week ; and for the benefit of any misguided admirers of Glasgow, the Prize List read :

  1st : One week's holiday in Paris.

  2nd : One week's holiday in Glasgow.

  3rd : *Two weeks'* holiday in Glasgow.

THE FARMER'S GRIEVANCE

John was aye complaining, but this year he was more vocal than usual as the harvest had been bad. Meeting his Parish Minister the conversation inevitably turned to the persistent troubles of the farmer.

"Well, John," the minister assured him, "you may have good cause to complain, but you must never forget that Providence looks after all things and even the birds of the air are provided for."

"Ay," replied John grimly, "aff my crops."

NON-TRADING AT A PROFIT

Stopping at a country farmhouse on a Sunday, a party of four motorists asked the farmer's wife if they could have glasses of milk. After some hesitation the milk was provided and greatly enjoyed. The motorists then asked about payment.

"Losh me!" said the horrified wife, "ye surely dinna think we sell milk on the Sabbath Day. You can just gie the bairns a half-croon each on your way oot!"

TAKING NO CHANCES

In a very small island in the very far North, ice-cream was a rare luxury. Once a year, however, a regular summer visitor to the island took with him a container of the delicacy sufficiently large to provide a special treat to all the islanders.

When the donor was on the point of leaving again for the mainland, he passed an old crofter, bent over his work, and asked him if he had had his share.

"No man," he replied, "that I have not."

"And why not?" returned the disappointed visitor, "there was, I am sure, enough and to spare for everybody."

"Weel now," came the studied reply, "I had it the once last year. But no this year. The once was enough. I dinna want it tae get a grip o' me like the tobacco."

A MAN OF PRINCIPLE

A North Country merchant with very strict views on business ethics was being pressed by a traveller for a city firm to accept a box of a hundred cigars as a Christmas gift. The merchant, however, sturdily refused the offer, declaring that he had never taken something for nothing and did not intend to begin now. After exhausting all his powers of persuasion, the traveller finally suggested that in order that the merchant should not violate his principle of never taking something for nothing he should offer him a sixpence for the box.

" Just give me a sixpence and nobody can say you have changed your ways. Come now, hand over the sixpence and here's the 100 cigars."

The problem in ethics being thus disposed of, the case now became one for the practical man and the multiplication table.

" Aweel," replied the steadfast but long-headed man of principle, " since ye put it that way, here's a shillin'. I may as weel hae the twa boxes when I'm at it."

RULES ARE RULES

Old Erchie had served the Railway Company as Guard on the local railway for nearly fifty years, and when his time to retire arrived he found the parting a severe wrench.

Hearing how keenly their old employee felt leaving the service, the Company arranged to present him with an old coach to keep at the bottom of his garden to serve as a daily reminder of his active days on the line.

One very wet day some of his friends called to see Erchie and were informed by his wife that he would be " on the train." Going down the garden they found Erchie sitting on the step of the carriage, smoking furiously at his pipe and with an old sack over his shoulders to protect him from the downpour.

" Hullo, Erchie," his friends greeted him, " why are ye no inside in a day like this ? "

" Can ye no see," replied Erchie with a nod towards the windows, " they only sent me a non-smoker ! "

SWEETS OF OFFICE

The scene was a quiet West Coast port. The small puffer was tied up at the jetty and a solitary figure in weather-beaten blue leaned reflectively over the side. To the approaching visitor—who knew his Neil Munro—the picture was vividly reminiscent of *Para Handy* and *The Vital Spark*. And of course the natural thing to do was to say how much he admired the ship.

After a preliminary greeting to attract the attention of the man on board, the visitor declared with what conviction he could muster, " Man, that's a very fine vessel you have there ! "

" She is that," came the reply, " a very fine ship indeed. Chust so ! "

After further exchanges regarding the merits of the vessel, the visitor ventured to ask, "And are you the Skipper ? "

" Well, now," was the cautious reply, " I don't know about being the Skipper, but I'm the one that gets the sugar in his tea ! "

NOTHING BUT THE TRUTH

The new arrival in the village was one who " kept hersel' tae hersel' " and did little to satisfy enquiries about her affairs. But one of her nearer neighbours persisted in her enquiries and would give her little respite.

After exhaustive and fruitless questions regarding her previous background and personal history, the affairs of the husband came under review.

"And where does your man work ? " was the next enquiry.

" Oh," was the reply, " in the district."

"Aye, aye," persisted the neighbour, " but jist *where* ? "

" Weel," was the cautious reply, " if you maun ken, it's in the Coonty."

The exchanges continued on these lines for some time until, by chance, it came to light that the husband had something to do with the roads. Feeling she was now near her goal, the inquisitive one was ready for the final thrust.

" On the roads, you say," she persisted, " but hoo much does he *make* ? "

" Oh," came the ready answer, " naething on wet days ! "

UNDUE ALARM

In one or other of the old collections a good story appeared illustrating the ludicrous figure sometimes cut by a much exasperated man.

When the River Clyde in the upper reaches could only take very small vessels, a small steamboat stuck in the mud near Renfrew, and the Skipper had reluctantly to wait for the rising tide and hope to get refloated.

Fuming and raging at the delay, he saw a little boy taking his toy bucket to the riverside for some water. This was enough to bring the Skipper's anger to boiling point. Leaning over the side of his vessel he roared : " Tak' wan bucket o' water oot this river afore I get afloat and I'll warm your lug ! "

FALSE COLOURS

Mac had been in London for some time, and was feeling very lonely and very homesick. What would he not give to see some of his own kith and kin?

Waiting for a bus one day in a crowded street, he was suddenly confronted by a figure resplendent in MacDonald tartan tie. Blood was thicker than water, and his heart leapt at the sight of a member of the clan, and he lost no time in making his approach.

"That's a grand MacDonald tartan tie you're wearing," he began.

But there was no response from the newcomer. Mac tried again.

"I see you're a MacDonald," he continued.

But his dream was shattered when the stranger replied, "Excuse plees!"

THE REALIST

Fishing in a deep part of the river, Donald suddenly lost his footing and fell headlong into the surging current. His wife was a witness of the accident and was in a great state of alarm. After struggling vainly in the water for some time the half-drowned Donald was able to clutch at the rocky bank and with an effort pull himself to dry ground.

His wife, running excitedly towards him, cried in her relief "Oh Donald, you maun thank Providence for your escape."

"Well, yes," replied the sodden spouse, "I will thank Providence chust as you say. But I was ferry clever myself!"

LIGHT DIET

It is a well-known fact that West Coasters are fond of their "Tatties and Herring," and some are fonder of the herring than the tatties.

Murdo was doing nobly at the tea table when he called to his wife for more.

"Noo, Murdo," she replied, "go canny, you've had twelve already."

"Well, well, maybe so," said Murdo, "but one of them was awful small!"

FIRST CLASS EXTRAVAGANCE

Having done a substantial amount of business with the Railway Company, a worthy merchant from the Buchan district had been presented, as was then the custom, with two First Class Return Tickets to London.

He immediately presented himself at the Stationmaster's office and demanded the difference in cash between the cost of the First Class and Third Class fares.

" Ye ken weel enough," complained the merchant, " that I never travel first class."

" Well," replied the Stationmaster, " it is all the same to the Railway Company whether you travel first or third class. You can, of course, travel third class if you prefer it that way."

" Nonsense, man," returned the merchant, " ye canna get away frae the fact that thae tickets entitle me and my wife to travel first class—and if we're content wi' third class, surely I'm entitled to the difference back."

" But," the official patiently explained, " you are under no obligation to go first class—and I will exchange your first class tickets for third class with pleasure. But you must see that no money can be returned when no money was paid ! "

The argument went on in this way for a long time, but the Stationmaster was emphatic that no cash would be refunded. At last the merchant gave it up.

" Aweel," he grumbled as he turned away, " I suppose I'll juist need to gang first class. But I ca' it nothing short o' damned extravagance ! "

PART THREE

WHAT'S THE JOKE?

1. NO LAUGHING MATTER

IT is a very risky business indeed to say anything at all about the theory of Humour and the Springs of Laughter.

If you are ever foolish enough to speak to your neighbour about a possible general principle you can expect nothing but black looks. All he wants to hear from you or anybody else on this abstract subject is a new concrete joke. If you are caught in an attempt to discover anything in the shape of a general formula to cover all mirth-provoking occasions, you are taken to be fit for any kind of spoil and on no account to be trusted. You will in fact be told very bluntly that your own Sense of Humour—which can never have been very lively—has now completely gone.

You are, then, given clearly to understand that no theorist in such a subject can possibly have any real appreciation of humour himself. How else could he keep a straight face in pausing to ask himself what he was up to. Imagine anybody solemnly labelling jokes, and in cold blood laying them out for inspection like fossils !

Voltaire, it seems, said the last word in pronouncing that the laugh is a sign of joy just as tears are a sign of pain ; and that anyone who pushes his curiosity further is a fool. After all, a good joke is a comparatively rare thing ; but the quickest way to kill one is to open it up and look inside. On no account must you inquire about ingredients.

Again, you will be told with a touch of impatience that all down the centuries, from the days of Aristotle, learned philosophers, psychologists and thinkers have been slapping their foreheads and knitting their brows over what they have called " this little problem " ; and in many solid volumes have already made their laborious pronouncements about the basic joke.

Other equally eminent specialists have given up the struggle altogether, frankly confessing that Humour appears in so many forms that it quite defies definition. It is too light a thing, too quick on its wing to be caught and examined. It is far too subtle, much too elusive for analysis. You can't lay hold of it or pin it down.

Why then, at this time of day, need we fash ourselves about what Humour is, and how it is and why it is? Perhaps it is just the prodding idea that, despite the dangers of analysis, it might add an edge and spice to the subtle qualities of our own National Humour if we have in very broad outline a reminder of what the more prominent among the authorities have said about Humour in general. The chances are that our appreciation of humour may be heightened if, in a flash of perception, we are able to " place " it in a class, seeing even as we laugh what we are laughing at. As we laugh we should have the added satisfaction of discerning a truth. For it can be claimed for the Scot that the more " head " there is in any humour, the more he likes it.

What then, very briefly indeed, have the acknowledged specialists to say about the Springs of Laughter? A preliminary examination of the main authorities seems to justify the conclusion that there are in fact not more than half a dozen different kinds of laugh in all. While laughter may spring from a compound of different factors, while several influences may combine, the theory is that one particular and predominant constituent can be noticed.

Having got thus far, it should do nobody any harm if some of the collected samples of expert opinion are labelled and examined, along with some familiar and less familiar Scottish specimens of humour which seem to illustrate each particular theory.

2. THE SIX LAUGHS

(i) THE LAUGHTER OF SUPERIORITY

THERE is a very impressive list of eminent and weighty authorities who advance the theory that there is a persistent and emphatic note of self-congratulation in all laughter. The joke, they insist, must be *on* somebody. No man laughs when he bumps his own funny bone. Nothing is funny unless it happens to someone else. At the spectacle of the misfortunes, the discomfitures, the flounderings, the " awkward fixes " of our neighbour—as he " puts his foot in it "—we are said to experience an agreeable sense of superiority and elevation. As the philosopher Hobbes has it, " we suddenly applaud ourselves." It takes a' sorts o' folk to mak' a world " we are saying, " but Thank Heaven I'm no' one o' them."

Plato was among the first to announce that this ungracious element of superiority and derision is behind all laughter,

" Ay, he's a dab **haun' at layin'** linoleum, is Andra . . ."

holding that we only laugh at the sight of another's misfortune. As Johnson put it—there can be no joy without inequality. Since that early day a long list of discerning judges have been nodding assent.

According to Hegel, laughter is little more than an expression of self-satisfied shrewdness. Swift agrees that men laugh at another's cost; and Hazlitt falls into line 'in affirming that someone is sure to be the sufferer by a joke. "What is sport to one," he says, "is death to another." As more modern specimens from a formidable list we find Max Beerbohm ready to wager that nine-tenths of the world's best laughter is laughter *at*, not *with*, and Swinnerton summing up to say that the loudest laugh, common to all the World, is caused by a tumble.

Ask yourself if you are laughing at another's hurt, if you are conscious of a feeling of superiority and "self-satisfied shrewdness," as you observe the figure cut by the victim in an example like this :

It was a wet Monday afternoon and Geordie Esslemont was in his best blacks, complete with stove-pipe hat and umbrella.

"Wha's funeral is't the day, Geordie ? " asked one of his cronies on meeting him in the High Street.

"It's the wife's mother," replied Geordie, with as sombre an expression as he could muster.

Two days later, Geordie was still in his blacks, but looking a bit befuddled and bedraggled, when he again encountered his friend in the High Street.

Again the question naturally arose,

"And wha's funeral is't this time Geordie ? "

"It's the wife's mother," again replied Geordie.

"But that was on Monday Geordie ! " continued his friend with a look of concern.

"Losh me," returned the suddenly sobered Geordie with a strange light in his eye, " nae wonder I'm hungry ! "

(ii) THE LAUGHTER OF SYMPATHY

It is not very difficult to produce a list of spokesmen who are ready to give a flat denial to the claims of the Superiority— Scorn—Derision School. They confidently assure us that laughter is genial and kindly, a friendly thing. It has in it nothing of the "proud self-comparer," no trace of animosity

THE LAUGHTER OF SYMPATHY

"Our Laughter binds us to him."

" Wullie's changed his mind—he's listenin' tae the broadcast
instead."

or the elements of scoffing and mockery. We do not laugh at or over our neighbour but to him and through his troubles with him. Our laughter binds us to him. There, we say, but for the Grace of God . . . We are not patronising with a self-satisfied sense of superior adaptation in this type of incident :—

It was a special occasion at the Castle and the Duke and Duchess were giving a dinner to their tenants. At the far end of the table sat a bluff old farmer obviously enjoying all the good fare provided.

In due course the dessert was served and, after his first spoonful, he thought the time had arrived for compliments to the Duchess.

" Ay, ma leddie," he shouted to the top of the table, " it's weel kenned wha was at the makin' o' *this* puddin'."

Roddie was the local Piper. It was his proud boast that he could play any tune you could name, although some of his critics would tell you that Roddie blew so lustily that all his tunes sounded alike.

The big night of the year had arrived and Roddie was playing his solo at the town " Store " Concert. He blew and skirled to some purpose and his selection was greeted with great applause. To the accompaniment of shouts of " encore " a voice was heard from the back of the hall, " Gie's ' Hieland Laddie' Roddie ! "

Roddie's smile of satisfaction suddenly disappeared, " What ! " he cried, " *Again ?* "

The secret source of humour, according to Mark Twain, is not joy but sorrow. Everything human is somehow pathetic, and laughter is but a " saddened smile of compassion " for our common lot. It springs from the contrast, as Leacock puts it, " between the fretting cares and petty sorrows of the day and the long mystery of tomorrow."

There will always be something of mild pity in our minds in meeting examples of this kind :

Old Mrs McFarlane, with some of her relatives, was visiting her husband's grave.

" Aye," she said, looking round the cemetery, " here we are. There's Willie Mackay, the grocer, and there's his wife. And here's ma Jeems—*jist the auld whist pairty.*"

(iii) THE LAUGHTER OF INCONGRUITY

From earliest times, from as far back as the days of Aristotle, there have been rabid advocates of the theory that at the root of all comic enjoyment there is the detection of some form of ugliness or distortion, some kind of blemish. Although they are said to have only " laughed lightly," the ancients found the spectacle of a dwarf or hunch-back the proper occasion for mirth.

While, these many centuries ago, even philosophers could laugh at physical deformity and the mis-shapen, the forms of ugliness which now amuse us are moral deformities or blemishes of character, some departure from the normal ways in which we as individuals look at the world.

In a word, there is occasion for laughter when there is some lapse from normal ideas. We laugh at the sudden perception of overstatement or understatement—whenever we detect something askew somewhere, something wrong with something. As the American Samuel Crothers sums it up in our own day, " Humour is the frank enjoyment of the imperfect,"—whether of something which looks queer, like the " funny face " or mask, or whether of an idea which strikes us as ludicrous as a mental image ; when, for instance, you see a picture of a naked savage in a silk hat.

We are, as in the following type of case, tickled by the topsy-turvy arrangement or clashing of ideas—by " uncommon mixtures."

The old West Country minister gave a choice example of the incongruous when he prayed that we might be spared the horrors of war, " especially as depicted in the *Illustrated London News* and *Graphic* " ; and when he went on later to refer to Sir Isaac Newton as being " as weel acquainted wi' the stars as if he had been born and brocht up among them."

We are also laughing at bizarre mixtures and incongruous juxtapositions, as in examples of this kind :

Wee Jeannie had been asked to sing at the Sunday School Soiree. It was only when she had mounted the platform that the chairman asked her what she would like to sing.

THE LAUGHTER OF INCONGRUITY

"The topsy-turvy arrangement of ideas."

"Understand once and for all—there is one thing I will *not* tolerate in this Regiment and that's *Fighting*!"

" I would like to sing two, sir," ventured Jeannie.

" All right, Jeannie," replied the chairman, " what are they to be ? "

" ' Jesus Loves Me '," answered the smiling Jeannie, " and ' Fu' the noo '."

(iv) THE LAUGHTER OF SURPRISE

If we had merely to count heads in reaching a verdict, we could almost decide at once that the joke of jokes, the common feature of every joke, is Surprise. The advocates of the theory of the unexpected would perhaps outnumber the sponsors of all alternative theories combined. The list of authorities in the Surprise Group is not only long and impressive, but it is significant that it also contains a larger proportion of the modern experts in the subject than can be found in support of any other theory.

A prominent name in the list is that of the American Max Eastman. As an indication of the trend of current opinion, he mentions the case of Mr Harold Horne, whom he describes as the leading joke-fancier in the United States. This Mr Horne, we are informed, has collected between one and two million jokes. Having sifted, sorted, and codified his collection, Mr Horne finds that jokes are the simplest things in the world. They all consist, he says, of " frustrated expectation."

Another modern American, Milton Wright, is equally convinced that all jokes can be boiled down and reduced to one.

" In every joke, jape, jest, or anecdote," he declares, " somebody must be surprised. Sometimes it is one of the characters involved in the story, and sometimes it is the hearer of the story.

In any case, there is a sudden, surprised recognition of a fact that had not been realised before. The dawning of that recognition is the grand-daddy of all jokes."

THE LAUGHTER OF SURPRISE

" Anyone . . . at variance with his profession."

" Ah'm afraid it's goin' tae be a bigger job than ah thocht . . ."

Going back two hundred years or so, Fielding, in subscribing to the Surprise theory, was saying that this element is particularly laughable when we discover anyone to be at variance with his professions, to be the opposite of what he affects. There is a strong appeal to laughter when we detect discrepancies between the real character and the assumed role—when we suddenly get a peep behind the mask, as in an instance of this kind :—

A vendor of quack medicines at one time plied his wares in Leith. Of doubtful nationality himself, he was always at some pains to pose as a Scot and to curry favour with his audience by making, in the course of his sales talk, some flattering allusions to famous Scotsmen.

"Ay, yes, my friends," he would say, "as our own Sir Robert the Burns used to say in his famous poem ' The Immortal Memory,' ' A man's a man—and a' for that ! ' "

So much for some specimen pronouncements from a few of the comparatively modern opinions. They do not of course pretend that they have made any sort of discovery. For it has all been said before. We find, for instance, that Cicero was saying it all centuries ago. Although he practically confessed his inability to say what laughter is he finally declared that in his opinion " cheated expectation " was at the root of it.

We are led on and " playfully disappointed." The listener is expectant, ready to assimilate a particular idea. The movement of his thought turns in one direction, but a sudden twist occurs. There is always this sharp smack of surprise in examples of this kind :—

The Inspector was on his annual visit to a Country School in the North. On being informed that the class had been studying Gray's " Elegy " he proceeded to put the pupils through their paces.

" The curfew tolls the knell of parting day," intoned the great man before addressing the class. " Now, children," he began, " can you tell me what a curfew is ? "

No reply came from the class. After a long pause the Inspector continued :

" Come, come now—surely you must know what a curfew is ! "

Still there was no response from the nervous pupils. At last the old schoolmaster could contain himself no longer :

" Ye lot o' stupid eediots," he cried in exasperation, " dae nane o' ye ken what a *whaup* is ? "

The above recalls another instance of the unexpected which is recounted in a Border town which cannot be far from Melrose.

The local message boy was on his rounds and one of the newer residents had, on this particular occasion, opened the door to receive the household supplies. Anxious to put the boy at his ease on seeing a comparatively new face he asked him his name.

" Walter Scott, sir," came the firm reply.

" Indeed, indeed," said the newcomer, " that is very interesting. Yours is a very well known name in these parts."

" Weel, sir," answered the boy proudly, " It *should* be. I've been delivering here for aboot three year ! "

(v) THE LAUGHTER OF RELIEF

There is another distinct group of specialists who have it that we laugh primarily because our fears are relaxed, and only secondarily because we are amused. Laughter, they say, is not always associated with amusement, although it may be tinged with it. Even if the situation has in it one or other of the ingredients of Superiority, Sympathy, Incongruity, or Surprise, we are informed that the main element in the laugh is a sense of release, a feeling of escape from some pressure or constraint.

Prominent among the later exponents of this theory is J. C. Gregory, the author of *The Nature of Laughter*. The passing of a crisis, he contends, always prepares a path for laughter. There is sheer relief or re-assurance in the laughter of the observer who watches a peril that passes him but touches another. " He laughs," as Cowper puts it, " at what he trembled at before." It is probably the same impulse which, as Scott says in his Journal, makes the birds sing when the storm has blown over.

Examples coming into this group were common during the worst of the 1940 Clydeside air raids.

" Talk aboot laugh," said one woman, relating her experience after a heavy raid. " My man's sister had been peyin' into the Friendly Society for fifteen years to get a richt burial—*and it took them ten days tae dig her oot !* "

Max O'Rell, in his *Friend Macdonald*, has recalled some choice examples in which a feeling of " release from tension " is the main ingredient.

He presents the Scottish picture of the solemn gathering for family prayers and the Master of the house, with great gravity and sincerity, making his supplications.

" O Lord," he proceeded, " O Lord, give us receptivity, that is to say, O Lord, the power of receiving impressions ! " [1]

The suggestion then, is that we are conscious of an agreeable feeling of sudden relaxation as the mind—having been occupied with something heavy—finds the focus suddenly diverted to something light. The sudden switch gives rise to an agreeable feeling of relief. In the ensuing laughter we are " refreshed by a sense of liberation."

This conception of the laughter of " the let go " is favoured by Kant and other thinkers and is the lang-nebbit way of saying anti-climax. Herbert Spencer, for instance, also lays it down that laughter is bound to result naturally when the attention is sharply transferred from great things to small, when there is some form of sudden intrusion of the droll into the domain of the serious.

The situation may have a hint of menace in it. A bit of trouble may seem to be brewing. Then comes the sudden change to a lighter level of interest as in instances of this kind :—

The little West Coast Pier was having a busy morning, as a small cargo vessel was landing timber.

The Skipper, anxious to be off again, was directing operations from the deck, when he observed that Roddie was taking two planks at a time while Donald was taking only one.

He shouted angrily to Donald :

" Don't you see, man, that Roddie is carrying two planks at a time ? "

" Indeed I do," replied Donald, " indeed I do. And I was meaning to speak to him about it myself."

---

[1] In commenting on the above specimen, the Frenchman adds :—

The entire Scotch character is there. What forethought, what cleverness, what a business-like talent ! To explain to God the significance of the far-fetched word *receptivity* so that He should not be able to say " There is a worthy Scotsman who uses outlandish words ; I do not know what he wants."

" Here, listen to this yin, Ella . . ."

(vi) THE LAUGHTER OF CORRECTION

Turning finally to the examination of our sixth exhibit, we are to observe at the outset that we are dealing this time with a function of laughter as well as its cause.

As a means of maintaining the customary and conventional, laughter is the deadliest of weapons. Nothing but what Lord Shaftesbury called " the handsome and just " is proof against it. Morally considered, says another essayist, it is next to the Ten Commandments. It unmasks and exposes all humbugs and extremes.

Society distrusts anything outlandish and must curb all oddness or breaches of the familiar. By what the poet Thomson calls " the dread laugh which scarce the firm philosopher can scorn," it brings its non-conforming members to heel and compels compliance with accepted codes. As Swift puts it, men are not lashed, but laughed out of their follies. All pomposities and affectations are laughed down as when we find Lord Auchinleck describing Dr Johnson as " ane that keepit a schule and ca'd it an Academy." Bubbles must be pricked.

Bergson is probably the leading advocate of this view, that Laughter, with its corrosive quality, serves as a sharp social discipline. He declares that we always find in Laughter an unavowed intention to humiliate and consequently to correct our neighbour. The quiet laugh in the following incident would, he says, be the laugh of Correction :

When Dr Cooper was minister in Aberdeen there was some discussion and concern as to his leanings in the direction of Anglican ritual. Having occasion to write Dr MacGregor of St. Cuthbert's, he headed his letter " Aberdeen—All Saints' Day," to receive a reply beginning " Edinburgh—Washing Day ! "

This is the philosopher's " Gay Rebuke," the laugh which Meredith in turn described as a safeguard against the overblown, affected, pretentious and bombastical. It is the equivalent of the slow handclap. We chastise with a laugh.

The following also seems to be the situation which the Bergsons and the Merediths have in mind.

A famous old Edinburgh Divine was being assisted on one occasion by a newly appointed but very young and very conceited assistant. In the vestry prior to the service his manner was particularly pompous and patronising. Finally, he put it to the Doctor, " I—ah—suppose, Doctah, you—ah—repeat—ah—the Lord's Prayer in some paht of—ah—the—sahvice ? "

" Ay, ay, to be sure," put in the Doctor, " unless ye ha'e a better ane o' your ain."

Having told us that first and foremost it is the part of laughter to castigate, Bergson proceeds to explain what he finds to be the basic joke. We laugh, he says, every time a person reminds us of a machine—of " something mechanical encrusted on the living." He sees the laughable when he finds anything in a human being that suggests some rigid mechanical action.

Bergson extends his theory to the mental field, holding that anything suggesting mechanical rigidity of mind or the behaviour of an automaton is laughable. In his " inelasticities " he includes absentmindedness, or obstinacy, as they remind the observer of something stereotyped, ready-made, or fixed, instead of " the pliant organism of the man." We laugh, he says, as they " clash with the inner suppleness of life."

If there is any portion of truth in the Bergson theory that rigidities and obstinacies are laughable, there ought to be many choice illustrations from the humour of a serious and perhaps stiff-necked people—as in this example.

The old Beadle had held office for the best part of a lifetime. As he lay on his deathbed he summoned his son to leave with him some parting words of advice.

" Listen to your auld faither, John," he said. " I've been beadle here for forty year and mair and I've been thinkin' that they may mak ye my successor. Well, my son, I've jist ane bit o' advice to gie ye."

After a long pause he finished with impressive gravity, " John, never forget this—*Resist a' impruvements.*"

3. CONCLUSION

SO much for the briefest review of what a few of the accepted authorities have to say about the Springs of Laughter.

After much reflection and furrowing of brows, the specialists of the different schools tell us what in their opinion is the one pervasive element, the one fundamental situation in every laugh. Behind all the variations it is always possible, they say, to identify the same original theme. In a word, there is one joke—and those who cannot see it are walking in darkness.

It seems that the partitions dividing the various groups are often very thin. But if we could confront an advocate of each theory with a random example of what in Scotland we accept as a mirth-provoking incident we would in fact get half a dozen distinct and separate reasons for the laugh.

Having taken our quick glance at the opinions of the experts, we ought now, perhaps, to be content to keep our distance and be satisfied with the simple conclusion that Humour is a funny thing. If we pushed our curiosity further and attempted to trace some thread or line common to them all, we should very soon find ourselves, like the puddock under the harrow, " wi' ower mony maisters."

It is enough, perhaps, to remember that it is, at anyrate, a good thing to laugh, and to hope that—to use the words of a historian of an earlier day—it can still be said of us :

" Among other good qualities, the Scot has been distinguished for humour—not for venomous wit, but kindly, genial humour, which half loves what it laughs at—and this shows clearly enough that those to whom it belongs have not looked too exclusively on the gloomy side of the world."